Journeys
Readings in the Academic Disciplines

First Edition

Carol Friend
Mercer County Community College

Laura Knight
Mercer County Community College

WINDSOR PRESS AND PUBLISHING, L.L.C.

Adelphia, New Jersey, United States

WINDSOR PRESS and PUBLISHING
PO BOX 248
ADELPHIA, NJ 07710-0248
windsorpp@att.net
http://windsorpress.net
(732) 577-6327

Printed in the United States of America

ISBN: 978-0-9837145-0-7

Table of Contents

Readings

Humanities

Social Sciences

Natural Sciences and Allied Health

~~~~~~

Copyright Acknowledgements

To the Instructor:

The objective of this book is to introduce first-year college students to readings in the academy. It is designed so students read and respond to texts from across the disciplines—the humanities, social sciences, and natural sciences—and include the type of readings they will encounter during their college years.

The book begins with "An Overview of Reading Skills and Strategies," which summarizes the main points of the thinking and reading process, including metacognition, schema, SQ3R, and Cornell Note taking.

A total of 33 readings, grouped by academic discipline, includes short stories, essays, narratives, poems and speeches. Each reading begins with "Activate your Schema" questions, followed by vocabulary found in the reading and noted by paragraph number. Students should look up these words and write the definitions in the margins if they are unable to glean the meanings from the context. While students are engaged in the reading, encourage them to interact with the text by highlighting, marking, taking notes and discussing it with others. Each reading ends with "Thinking and Responding to the Reading," which asks critical and creative-thinking questions. You can choose to have students use these questions for classroom discussion or as writing assignments. These questions advance their critical reading and thinking skills. By repeatedly answering and discussing the points in these questions, your students' skills will improve.

Some of the readings are quite short while others are longer. The length of the readings, however, is not an indicator of their difficulty. You can choose to read the selections by discipline, theme, or ease of reading level.

The last two pages offer a list of quotes from significant thinkers along with a list of commonly confused words and their spellings. We specifically offer the list of quotes as a springboard for discussions and web research.

To the Student:

 We designed *JOURNEYS: Readings in the Academic Disciplines* with the expectation that reading across the disciplines will complement and reinforce your understanding of the academy. Colleges throughout the country require undergraduate students to take courses across three major academic areas: the humanities—works that are man-made, such as art, music, dance and literature; the social sciences—how groups of people interact; and the natural sciences—the world of nature that man does not control. To be a citizen of the world, you must learn to be a reader in all three areas, and this text will help you to achieve that goal.

The primary objective of this text is to help you improve your understanding of the world in which you live, increase your vocabulary, expand your understanding of what is expected of you as an undergraduate student in college, and sharpen your thinking about, and interaction with, textbooks.

Students often do not realize the important role they play as readers. Without readers there would be no need for writers. We readers are in conversation or dialogue with the writer. All writing responds to an expectation that someone is on the other end to receive the message. While examining the following poem "Catch," by Robert Francis, see if you "catch" the relationship that he describes.

Two boys, uncoached, are tossing a poem together,
Overhand, underhand, backhand, sleight of hand,
   every hand,
Teasing with attitudes, latitudes, interludes, altitudes,
High, make him fly off the ground for it, low, make him stoop,
Make him scoop it up, make him as-almost-as-possible miss it,
Fast, let him sting from it, not, now fool him slowly,
Anything, everything tricky, risky, nonchalant,
Anything under the sun to outwit the prosy,
Over the tree and the long sweet cadence down,
Over his head, make him scramble to pick up the meaning,
And now, like a posy, a pretty one plump in his hands.

Did you get the main point of this poem? Great. You know that the game is a metaphor for the relationship between readers and writers. Francis is describing that interactive process we call reading.

In *JOURNEYS: Readings in the Academic Disciplines* you will be responsible for thinking, reading, responding and interacting with the readings in this textbook. To accomplish this, first do an overview of the book by examining all of its parts.

As you examine the Table of Contents, take note that the readings are divided into three academic areas: humanities, social sciences and natural sciences.

"Overview of Reading Skills and Strategies" is an overview and review of reading skills and strategies that you can return to over and over to increase your reading comprehension, study skills and critical thinking skills.

Before each reading, you are asked preview questions, called "Activate Your Schema," to get you thinking about the main point of the reading. Jot your thoughts down right after the preview questions, and then at the end of the reading, go back and look at your initial response. Ponder whether after reading and learning about the topic, you have the same understanding or a deeper understanding and whether you agree or disagree with your initial thoughts.

Before each reading is a vocabulary list with the paragraph number where the words appear. With each word, try to see if you can figure out the unfamiliar word's meaning by its context. If not, look up the words you don't know the meanings of to improve your comprehension of the reading as well as to increase your college-level vocabulary. Put those meanings in the margin where the word appears in the reading so that when you come across the new word, you already have the meaning in a note. You can continue to read without a break while incorporating the new word into your mind. This method will increase your reading rate and comprehension.

Before reading the piece, it's a good idea to look at the comprehension questions that follow the reading to help guide your interactive reading process. Then, while reading, have a pen or highlighter handy to mark interesting points to remember and to organize the main ideas, supporting points, and details. Additionally, write in the margins as a way to remember and respond to the comprehension questions that you've already read.

Your professor may ask you to write your responses or discuss them with classmates. Both are important in checking your own understanding of the reading. Also, it is important to hear and respond to others' understanding of the readings assigned by your professor.

The last two pages offer a list of quotes from significant thinkers along with a list of commonly confused words and their spellings. Your instructor may assign all or parts of this list of quotes as a springboard for discussion and web research.

The readings in *JOUNEYS: Readings in the Academic Disciplines* are short and long, about the United States and other countries and cultures, fiction and non-fiction; they are the type of material that college students read. Although you may be familiar with some of these readings, reading them with your new skills will open your eyes to meanings and connections you did not notice before. Welcome to the wonderful world of reading where you will glean information, spark your imagination and broaden your ideas.

An Overview of Reading Skills and Strategies

　　Before you settle at your desk to start reading, you need to learn how to read at the college level. Of course you know how to decode the words on the page; however, college reading differs from reading for pleasure, such as with magazine or beach reading. Below are the proven strategies to help you read college-level material and prepare for exams and papers.

Metacognition

　　Metacognition is the self-regulating process of reading comprehension. *Meta* means aware and *cognition* means knowledge or knowing. To use your metacognition, step outside of your distractions and instead concentrate on the words on the page. You were probably taught to "read with your eyes only" but, in fact, you really read with your mind, and your mind makes the meaning from the text. Developing your meta-cognition is a great way to ensure that you understand what you are reading. As your metacognition develops, your comprehension problems will lessen because your mind and eyes will be working together to interact effectively with the text.

Schema

　　Schema refers to your accumulated prior knowledge and experiences that help you navigate the world. When readers rely on past experiences or background knowledge—schema—the reading is more interesting, enjoyable and easier to understand. Readers with a great deal of past reading experiences grasp the meanings of new or unfamiliar topics more quickly than readers who seldom read. As you get in the habit of using your schema, your reading comprehension and enjoyment of reading will improve.

Inference

　　An inference is an implied meaning arising out of what is suggested but not directly stated in the text. Inference is also known as reading between the lines. Readers reach conclusions on the basis of evidence and reasoning provided or implied by the writer. Being able to understand inferences is an important thinking skill all readers must develop.

Worldview Perspective

Everyone has an overall perspective from which he/she sees and interprets the world. Every writer has a view of the world and of the subject matter about which he/she writes. As readers, we need to think about the point of view of the author. This is also called author's perspective. Once you understand the author's viewpoint, you can follow his/her thesis or argument and determine if your perspective or point of view is the same or different. By determining your point of view and the author's point of view, you are actively engaged in the reading and thinking process.

Purpose

We read texts differently depending on our purpose. To establish your purpose, you must first figure out your reading goal. Are you reading for enjoyment, to find specific information, to learn how to do something, to compare it with another reading or because you will be tested on the information? You should know this before you start readings. Also, you should look at the questions that most textbooks have following the reading. These questions may help you to see your purpose, especially if your instructor has assigned them. Once you have established your purpose, remember to use your metacognition and your schema skills.

Predict

Any thinking process, including thinking when reading, begins with what the subject is and what you think is going to happen to the subject. Based on the information in the text that you are given, you make an educated guess as to what will happen. If your prediction is close to what actually happens, then you know that you are actively thinking about the material and accurately comprehending the author's points. In addition, if your predictions about the topic or details contained in the reading are close to what happens in the reading, then you are more apt to retain the material. When you read metacognitively, activate your schema, establish your purpose, and make educated guesses while reading, then you are on your way to greater reading comprehension and reading ease.

SQ3R: Survey, Question, Read, Review, Respond, Review

Learning SQ3R technique is helpful when you read college textbooks.

Survey: Look at the title of the reading. This may be the title of the book or the title of the chapter, depending on your assignment. You should also look at the headings and subheadings, first sentence in each paragraph, captions under any pictures, any charts/graphs/maps, and bold or italic words.

Question: Reading interactively requires formulating questions either in the margin of the book or in your mind of who, what, where, why, when and how ("the 5 W's") about the reading. You do this to interact with the text. You can turn the title, headings or first sentences into questions. For example, if the chapter heading is "Causes of the American Revolution," you can turn it into questions: **What** were the causes of the American Revolution? **How** many causes were there? **Why** was there an American Revolution? **Who** was involved? **Where** did the events connected to the main causes take place? You should also ask yourself what your professor has said about the material or subject and what you already know about the subject.

If you are consciously searching for the answers to these questions while reading, you will better understand the material and retain in your memory what you read. You also stay hooked into the reading, much the same way you are hooked into a conversation when you actively ask questions.

Read: With pen or highlighter in hand, read the text interactively. The specific methods of reading interactively are in the next section.

Respond: The more senses you use, the more likely you are to remember the material for writing a paper or taking a test, examination or quiz. Reread the material, say the material aloud, hear the material, and write notes.

Review: There are many ways to review; here are a few ways. Look over your notes and what you have marked in the text. Make flashcards and test yourself. Cover your notes and ask yourself questions. You should do these right after you have read the material, but also periodically after this to cement the material into your mind, especially if the material will be on an upcoming quiz, test, or final examination.

Reading and Study Strategies

Marking the text

Always grab a pen or pencil before you start to read. Write directly in the book, usually in the margin. Although this may go against everything you've been taught about books, marking the text while you read is not only all right, but it is one of the most important steps in your understanding of the material. Marking the text will help you stay focused and actively engaged with the author's words, thoughts, and ideas. A connection will be established between you and the text. In marking text you are exercising the interactive critical reading process.

You may be tempted to underline many passages or words with a highlighter. However, you should use care with highlighting so that only the important ideas—not most of the text—is accented.

Here is a chart of some of the markings you may want to use in this and your other textbooks:

Mark	Meaning
_____	Underline the main idea or thesis
1, 2, 3 ...	Number major supporting details
?	I don't understand this; ask the professor
!	What?!? This material is surprising. Ask about this.
*	Note this; it is important.

Now, when you are in class, the important passages or the confusing passages or the surprising passages will stand out and you'll be able to ***contribute to*** and ***understand*** the discussion of the piece. When you are home sitting down to study for a test or to write an essay, you will be able to quickly find the important information you noted.

Note-Taking

Taking notes while reading a textbook will keep you actively engaged in the dialogue you are having with the author. First you identify the main points and terms necessary to know; be sure to include them in your notes. Explain each term or main point in either the margin of your textbook or in a formal style such as Cornell Note-Taking, outlining or mapping.

Note-taking may take longer than simply marking the text, but it will directly reinforce what you are reading. By taking notes, you strengthen your comprehension and provide the most direct way to remember the material for examinations.

There are several note-taking systems, both for lectures and textbooks. One of the most useful is the **Cornell Note-Taking Method**. Below is an example of Cornell Notes from a textbook chapter. When you are in class taking lecture notes, you apply these same steps.

Cornell Note-Taking Method

Directions:
1. Draw a line or fold your paper so that you have a column 2-3 inches wide on the left side. This column is for key words and phrases. Then create a 5-6-inch column to the right of the vertical line or fold. This section is for summary sentences, definitions or explanations that help clarify the key words and phrases you listed on the left.
2. To decide what to write on the right side of the line corresponding to the key words and phrases, ask yourself, "What have I read?" and "What are the most important ideas here?" Try to phrase the definition or explanation in your own words. However, if you are trying to memorize terms and concepts, then it is better to quote the material right from the textbook.

9

3. Review by covering what you have written on the right side of the line and saying in your own words, aloud, the answers to questions, facts or ideas based on the words or phrases uncovered on the left.

Here's an example of Cornell Note-Taking:

Activate schema	Use my frame of reference or past experiences to make the new ideas easier to understand
Establish purpose	Understand why I need to know this material
Inference	Draw conclusion based on reasons and evidence. "Read between the lines."

Language Awareness

Vocabulary Words in Context

One challenge in reading is new vocabulary. Here are some ways to unravel the meaning of an unfamiliar word or words. Vocabulary words in context means you can make an intelligent guess at the meaning of the word from the gist of the words around it. It's best not to interrupt your reading process to look up every unknown word right away in the dictionary. Mark unfamiliar words and then try these steps for making an educated guess at the meaning as you go. You'll acquire some real understanding of how words are used rather than just learning long vocabulary lists. Eventually you will confirm your guesses with a dictionary.

1. First, **SOUND** the word out. Use simple phonics to attempt saying it; try a couple of ways. You might recognize the word when you hear it.
2. Next, look at the **CONTEXT**. Guess at the word's meaning from the way it is used in the sentence. You may find that an informal

definition is worked in near the word, or maybe you will see the meaning reflected in the next idea, or you may just be able to determine its meaning by the way the passage continues.

3. If you can't understand what you're reading after using the above steps, pause and turn to the **DICTIONARY**; also, the textbook may have a glossary list. When you find your word, skim through the whole entry and find the most relevant meaning. Check the pronunciation, too.

4. Then reinforce your understanding by writing a usable, brief definition or synonym in the margin of your reading.

5. When you stop after a section of reading to make notes, check meanings of any words that are still unclear.

Connotation and Denotation

From Latin *de* meaning "apart" and *notatio/notationis* meaning "marking," denotation is the literal meaning of a word; think of it as the "dictionary meaning." Connotation comes from the Latin *con* meaning "together" and *notatio/notationis* meaning "marking"; connotations contain the positive and negative associations of a word.

You should be aware of the connotation of words while you read; you'll get a sense of the writer's point of view and you will discover the inferences and literary devices the writer uses to advance the meanings. Good readers can spot the differences between the connotation and the denotation of a word. For example, the simple word "home" is literally a building for humans to live in; this is its denotation. It also carries the connotation of comfort, security, and memories. Did you ever notice that advertisers use "home" more than "house"? This is because the connotations associated with home are more positive.

When you read, highlight or note in the margin the connotations you find; this will help improve your understanding of what the author is saying.

Literary Devices

Writers of both fiction and non-fiction frequently use literary devices to express meaning that goes beyond the words' ordinary meaning.

Figurative language uses words to convey a picture in our heads. The two most common ones are simile and metaphor.

A **metaphor** makes a direct comparison of two unlike things. For example, "love is a rose" explains love is beautiful and sweet-smelling but also has thorns.

A **simile** makes a comparison of two unlike things using "like" or "as." For example, "Her muscles were as hard as rocks" lets the reader understand how strong she is by this comparison.

Satire uses humor or wit to make a constructive point; its purpose is to edify through humor. Sarcasm, often confused with satire, uses words to mean the opposite of what is really meant, specifically to insult.

Foreshadowing offers hints and clues about what will come later in the reading.

Irony is the use of words to express something different from and often opposite to their literal meaning. Irony is often the absurdity between the actual result of a sequence of events and the normal or expected result. Writers who are satirists often use irony.

Tone is the writer's attitude toward the material that helps the reader hear the voice of the writer or character. You can figure out the tone by the writer's word choice. Tone may be playful, formal, ironic, serious, humorous, and so on.

Theme is general idea, message, or moral of a story.

Readings

from *Anatomy of a Murder*

Robert Traver

Activate Your Schema: Do you think lawyers should be able to use any means available to get their defendant released?

Vocabulary

irked (par. 4)	catharsis (par. 8)	rhetoric (par. 9)
blithely (par. 4)	anarchy (par. 8)	buttress (par. 9)

Note: This excerpt from the novel begins when the Lieutenant, who has been charged with murdering Barney Quill, is in jail talking with his lawyer about the plea the lawyer wants to use during the trial. The lawyer narrates this section.

1   "It's a pretty unscientific thing," my man the Lieutenant said thoughtfully. "This insanity business is pretty damned unscientific."

2   "Why do you say that?"

3   "Well, we can't prove insanity without a medical expert, you tell me. Yet you and I have already decided I was insane, we know that we're going to plead insanity—you tell me it's the only legal defense I've got. And even I can see that now. In other words you a mere lawyer and I a dumb soldier have between us decided that I was medically and legally insane. Having decided that, we must now go out and shop around for a medical expert to confirm our settled conclusion. Yet you tell me an ordinary medical doctor won't do." The Lieutenant shook his head. "It all sounds damned unscientific to me."

4   It irked me unaccountably to hear this Mister Cool so blithely undertake to criticize my profession. It was all right if a member of the family did, but for a perfect stranger... "Lieutenant," I said, "the easiest thing in the world is for a layman to poke fun at the law. Lawyers and the law are sitting ducks for ridicule and always have been. The average layman may in all his lifetime collide with but one small branch of the law, which he understands but imperfectly. He usually knows whether he won or lost. He may also remember

15

that Dickens, grumbling through Mr. Bumble[1], once called the law an ass. So for him all the law is henceforth an ass, and, overnight, he becomes its severest critic."

5   "But I still don't get it," the Lieutenant said. "On this score at least, the law looks like a prime ass."

6   "Granted," I said. "But the point I wish to make is that from this people may not safely proceed to damn all law. You of all men should be grateful that the massive structure known as the law really exists. It so happens that it represents your only hope."

7   "How do you mean?" the Lieutenant said, bristling.

8   "I'll try to tell you," I said. "Mr. Bumble was only partly right. He was only part right because, for all its lurching and shambling imbecilities, the law—and only the law—is what keeps our society from bursting apart at the seams, from becoming a snarling jungle. While the law is not perfect, God knows, no other system has yet been found for governing men except violence. The law is society's safety valve, its most painless way to achieve social catharsis; any other way lies anarchy. More precisely, Lieutenant, in your case the law is all that stops Barney Quill's relatives from charging in here and seeking out and shooting up every Manion on sight. It is also what would keep the heavily mortgaged Manions of Dubuque from in turn coming a-gunning for the Quills, in other words what keeps the fix you're now in from fanning out into a sort of Upper Peninsula version of Hatfield-McCoy."

9   I paused, warming to my unfamiliar role as a defender of law. "The law is the busy fireman that puts out society's brush fires; that gives people a *nonphysical* method to discharge hostile feelings and settle violent differences; that substitutes orderly ritual for the rule of tooth and claw. The very slowness of the law, its massive

---

[1]In Charles Dickens' *Oliver Twist*, Mr. Bumble is an official of the church who takes young Oliver Twist from the "baby farm" of the poor to the adult workhouse of the poor.

[2]The Hatfields and McCoys were two families who lived on the West Virginia-Kentucky border and feuded for many years. Over a dozen men were killed between the two families.

impersonality, its insistence upon proceeding according to settled and ancient rules—all this tends to cool and bank the fires of passion and violence and replace them with order and reason. That is a tremendous accomplishment in itself, however a particular case may turn out. As someone has well said, 'The difference between an alley-fight and a debate is law.'" I paused. "What's more, all our fine Magna Cartas and constitutions and bills of rights and all the rest would be nothing but a lot of archaic and high-flown rhetoric if we could not and did not at all times have the *law* to buttress them, to interpret them, to breathe meaning and force and life into them. Lofty abstractions about individual liberty and justice do not enforce themselves. These things must be reforged in men's hearts every day. And they are reforged by the law, for every jury trial in the land is a small daily miracle of democracy in action."

 Thinking and Responding to the Reading

1.   What is the lawyer's overall argument as presented in paragraph 9?
2.   What examples does he give to support this argument?
3.   What prescriptive and descriptive assumptions does the lawyer make about our laws?
4.   The law is presumed to provide its society with reasoned, logical arguments, not only to provide answers that are true. How does the author explain this?
5.   If you were a juror on this trial, what worldview perspectives would you rely on?

Angels on a Pin: A Modern Parable

Alexander Calandra

Activate Your Schema: Have you ever disagreed with an assignment or grade that a teacher gave you? Did you challenge it?

Vocabulary

colleague (par. 1)   barometer (par. 2)   lark (par. 12)
arbiter (par. 1)   pedantic (par. 12)   Sputnik (par. 12)

1   Some time ago, I received a call from a colleague who asked if I would be the referee on the grading of an examination question. He was about to give a student a zero for his answer to a physics question while the student claimed he should receive a perfect score and would if the system were not set up against the student. The instructor and the student agreed to an impartial arbiter, and I was selected.

2   I went to my colleague's office and read the examination question: "Show how it is possible to determine the height of a tall building with the aid of a barometer."

3   The student had answered: "Take the barometer to the top of the building, attach a long rope to it, lower the barometer to the street, and then bring it up, measuring the length of the rope. The length of the rope is the height of the building."

4   I pointed out that the student really had a strong case for full credit since he had answered the question completely and correctly. On the other hand, if full credit were given, it could well contribute to a high grade for the student in his physics course. A high grade is supposed to certify competence in physics, but the answer did not confirm this. I suggested that the student have another try at answering the question. I was not surprised that my colleague agreed, but I was somewhat surprised that the student did.

5   I gave the student six minutes to answer the question, with the warning that his answer should show some knowledge of physics. At the end of five minutes, he had not written anything. I asked if he

wished to give up, but he said no. He had many answers to this problem, he was just thinking of the best one. I excused myself for interrupting him and asked him to please go on. In the next minute, he dashed off his answer, which read: "Take the barometer to the top of the building and lean over the edge of the roof. Drop the barometer, timing its fall with a stopwatch. Then using the formula $S = \frac{1}{2} gt2$, calculate the height of the building.

[6]   At this point, I asked my colleague if he would give up. He conceded and gave the student almost full credit.

[7]   In leaving my colleague's office, I recalled that the student had said he had other answers to the problem, so I asked him what they were. "Oh, yes," said the student, "there are many ways of getting the height of a tall building with the aid of a barometer. For example, you could take the barometer out on a sunny day and measure the height of the barometer, the length of its shadow, and the length of the shadow of the building, and by the use of simple proportion, determine the height of the building."

[8]   "Fine," I said, "and what are the others?"

[9]   "Yes," said the student, "There is a very basic measurement method that you will like. In this method, you take the barometer and begin to walk up the stairs. As you climb the stairs, you mark off the length of the barometer along the wall. You then count the number of marks, and this will give you the height of the building in barometric units. A very direct method.

[10]   "Of course, if you want a more sophisticated method, you can tie the barometer to the end of a string, swing it as a pendulum, and determine the value of 'g' at the street level and at the top of the building. From the difference between the two values of 'g,' the height of the building can, in principle, be calculated.

[11]   "Finally," he concluded, "there are many other ways of solving this problem. Probably the best," he said, "is to take the barometer to the basement and knock on the superintendent's door. When the superintendent answers, you speak to him as follows: 'Mr. Superintendent, here I have a fine barometer. If you will tell me the height of this building, I will give you this barometer.'"

[12]   At this point, I asked the student if he really did not know the conventional answer to this question. He admitted that he did, but said that he was fed up with high school and college instructors trying to teach him how to think, to use the "scientific method" and

to explore the deep inner logic of the subject in a pedantic way, as is often done in the new mathematics, rather than teaching him the structure of the subject. With this in mind, he decided to revive scholasticism as an academic lark to challenge the Sputnik-panicked classrooms of America.

Thinking and Responding to the Reading

1. Why does the narrator's colleague need a referee? What is at issue? What is Calandra's main point?
2. Discuss the dilemma of the physics professors. Why are they uncomfortable giving the student full credit?
3. What is the student's reason for answering the question as he does?
4. The student uses both divergent and convergent thinking. Diagram both thinking steps.
5. Give the definition of creative and critical thinking. Did the student successfully solve the problem? Explain your answer.

Aunt Jim

Noreen Duncan

Activate Your Schema: There are people who have to hide who they are or change how they act because of the culture or society in which they live. Do you know any such people?

Vocabulary

vexed (par. 2)	fete (par. 4)	plantains (par. 5)
wooing (par. 2)	fortnight (par. 5)	wafted (par. 5)

1   She wore brown canvas and rubber-soled half boots; you know the ones the older children called gym boots. That's how she got her name: Aunt Jim. She lived with Aunt Lil in Aunt Lil's house, and the children loved Aunt Lil and her house, and they loved spending the August holidays with Aunt Lil. They loved waking up early to Aunt Lil's humming and singing, her tinkly little laugh, the smell of breakfast, salt fish and fried bakes and fresh chocolaty cocoa tea, with cinnamon and frothy milk. They spent the mornings catching lizards, sometimes *battymamselles*, or the nasty little ravine fish, *guabines*. While Aunt Lil did the ladies' hair and cooked lunch, Aunt Jim cleaned the yard, picked green mangoes and ceries and guavas for them, and drew perfect circles in the dirt for them to pitch marbles. Then she sat in the gallery and watched; she didn't watch Aunt Lil or the ladies or the children or anybody really, she just watched. She didn't say anything. After lunch, breadfruit, zaboca, shrimp or fish, Aunt Lil and Aunt Jim went into the bedroom, and they closed the door.

2   The children, tired and full of country food, would fall asleep, dreaming about the sea or the river, or Tarzan and Jane. In the afternoons, Aunt Jim walked behind the children, with a stick, as they went, single file, down the road and to the beach, and she sat on the beach and watched. She never said anything, but the children enforced her rules. If one pushed another's head underwater and held him, he would come up red-eyed and spitting salt: "Don't do that, boy. You want Aunt Jim to get vexed or what?" Then, as it

grew dark, Aunt Lil and Aunt Jim sat in the gallery, and the children would doze off to the sounds of their voices, swirling and darting and swooping around as the moths and candle flies, chasing and wooing around the lamp flame.

3   Aunt Lil's tinkly little laugh and her sweet smell filled the children's days and their night sleep. She smiled and sang and wore an apron with flowers, and a hibiscus over her ear in her hair, which curled a little around her neck. She talked and laughed with everybody—the ladies whose hair she did in the drawing room, and the fish sellers, and the hops bread man. On Sundays, she took the children and many of the neighbour children to church. Aunt Jim did not go to church. She sat in the gallery and waited until they came back, and after Aunt Lil had taken off her hat, her high heels, her pretty dress, she and Aunt Jim ate breakfast then, and drank strong country coffee together. In the afternoon, they went to a matinee, Aunt Lil and Aunt Jim.

4   Aunt Jim's face and features were perfect, perfectly oval eyes, neat little nose and mouth, but she did something with the muscles of her face, something that didn't make her look pretty at all, at all. Her forearms were large and well-developed, one could imagine, if she and Aunt Lil went to a carnival fete, Aunt Jim would put her arm around Aunt Lil's small waist, pulling her to her, hard, and dance close, one arm around Aunt Lil, the other hanging down. But that never happened. It could never happen.

5   The husband of Aunt Jim's sister died suddenly, and Aunt Jim went to see about her. She never came back. Nobody asked where she was or when she was coming back. Nobody said anything about her. And the children grew big and couldn't spend all of their August holidays at Aunt Lil's, but they still loved her and she them; they always came to spend a week or a fortnight or so, bringing their friends from their high schools. Aunt Lil baked and iced cakes and made jams and sweets then; she didn't do hair anymore. The children woke late to the smell of her breakfasts, the plantains fried, the new sweet bread, the coconut bake and the sounds of her singing and humming as she boiled fudge and made sugar cakes, and boiled the country coffee. All day people came by to pick up black cakes and bottles of guava jam, and Aunt Lil's tinkly little laugh and her sweet smell wafted through the house.

6   The children and their friends went down to the beach by

themselves when they felt like it. But every now and then, when one would shove another's head under water, and he would come up red-eyed and salt spitting, he would say, "Don't do that, boy. You want Aunt Jim to get vexed or what?" Then one of the friends would ask, "Who is Aunt Jim?" And one of the children would say, "*Cheups.* Don't bother with him. He is always bringing up old jokes."

Thinking and Responding to the Reading

1. Describe Aunt Lil physically
   a. first by listing the observations Duncan gives and
   b. then by what you can infer from these observations.
2. Describe Aunt Jim physically
   a. first by listing the observations Duncan gives and
   b. then by what you can infer from these observations.
3. Duncan implies a deeper relationship between the two women. What is this relationship? Where in the reading did you find this implication?
4. In paragraph 4, the narrator says, "It could never happen." To what is the narrator referring? Why could this never happen at this place and time?
5. What worldview perspective and values do Aunt Jim and Aunt Lil face from their culture?

The Bamboo Grove

Hai-Tao Tang

Activate Your Schema: What is your relationship with nature? Do you love it, ignore it, or take it for granted?

Vocabulary

serenity (par. 1)	vitality (par. 4)	pensive (par. 6)
cicadas (par. 2)	diligence (par. 4)	perseverance (par. 6)
manifest (par. 3)	vicariously (par. 5)	introspection (par. 6)

1   I like bamboo. For three and a half years, I took a walk in the bamboo grove by the Tanshui River in Taipei at dusk, almost every day, except when the weather was terribly bad, or when I had an important engagement such as tutoring a high school student or attending an important party. An hour-long walk in the grove provided me with great serenity and a time to reflect on myself and the things that happened during the day.

2   I like nature better than human society. Though at times I went there with a friend, most of the time I went there alone. While walking, I was in no mood for talking. I enjoyed listening to the soothing sounds of the bamboo leaves rustling in the wind, the chirping sounds of the returning birds, the shrilling sounds of mating cicadas and the rippling sounds of the river water.

3   At those times, I felt peace and harmony inside. At dusk, the color of the sky changed rapidly; the slanting sun's golden gleam would shine upon the river and make the water glitter, but soon the clouds near the sun would turn to orange, rose, and then gradually fade into purplish grey. In the meantime, these colorful clouds would manifest themselves in all kinds of strange shapes, allowing me to fantasize with imagination. In springtime, when the frozen earth began to thaw, grass started boring through the hard ground, and the bamboos became greener and more moist. After a heavy rainfall, the bamboo shoots would mushroom right in front of my eyes. What a sight! And the smell of life they gave forth was pleasant and refreshing, beyond any verbal description. I like bamboo.

⁴ I first noticed this place in the spring of my freshman year in college. Since then it soon became the favorite place for me to linger about. That spring my health improved quickly after a long illness, for which I had been discharged from military service the previous year. It was the vitality of nature that helped me to regain my health and my self-confidence. I could spend half an hour watching old men on boats fishing, marveling at the remarkable skill of these fishermen in catching fish and the strong will of the fish struggling to break away from the fishing line. When I walked on the path in the bamboo grove, I took great care not to step on earthworms, ants or other tiny insects. I admired them for their diligence and pitied them for their hardships in life. We were all a part of the great nature, after all.

⁵ Summer time brought many children out to swim in the river, and I enjoyed with them vicariously. The "gu-gu" sounds of frogs were also amusing. Obviously these poor musicians did not care whether their music was pleasing to human ears; they just enjoyed themselves. A man in his late thirties or early forties also came to the grove every day, and we nodded to each other whenever we met on our ways. He always carried a bamboo flute and occasionally played with it; the sound of it was somewhat saddening. He often chanted poems to himself, but in most cases he was just repeating the same poem, composed by Wang Han, a poet in the eighth century:

> Vintage wine in a jade cup, glittering at night
> I want to keep drinking, but the guitars on the horse back
> were calling the fight.
> Don't laugh at me should I lie drunken on the battle ground,
> Since antiquity, how many actually returned from war-
> bound?

He must have been a soldier away from home. I felt sad but didn't have the heart to ask because I was one, too.

⁶ In the fall my mood was generally more pensive. The grass turned yellowish and dry. The bamboos would shed some of their shells, and these shells would tumble in the wind, like wanderers with nowhere to go. Autumn was the time for reservation and perseverance. A brisk walk would energize my body and clear my mind. The poem-chanting, lonely man stopped coming while I kept my daily routine, as if visiting an ailing old friend. Observing from a distance the bustling vehicles and people going one way or the other

on the Ying Bridge, which was built to cross the Tanshui River, was a sobering thing: human lives did not differ from those of the busy ants and bees, after all. I would then heave a sigh. I was one of them too; I needed some time for introspection.

7   Winter time in Taipei is characterized by days of continuous rain. I went to the grove only when the weather allowed me, usually twice or three times a week. There was no one else roaming. In solitude, I felt I was ever stronger standing in the cold wind. Only the bamboos remained there solemnly; they were my true friends. I like bamboo.

8   This was over forty years ago, and I was then in my early twenties. Things have changed drastically since that time. When I revisited the site in the summer of 1983, I could not find a single bamboo there. All the bamboos had been cut down, and the entire place had been turned into a training ground of a driving school. I regretted very much the change that had taken place. But who knows? I might be wrong. Maybe youngsters nowadays do not need a quiet place to walk around and do some soul-searching. They may prefer driving around in a fancy car instead.

 Thinking and Responding to the Reading

1. Tang uses many of the five senses to make observations. List an example for each sense.
2. How does Tang interpret nature? Use specific examples or details he supplies.
3. List three facts Tang presents.
4. Is it a reasonable conclusion for the author to say that the bamboos were his "true friends"? Explain your answer in a few sentences.
5. Would you argue that nature plays an important role in your life? Explain your answer.

Capital Punishment

Carl Wellman

Activate Your Schema: Are you for or against capital punishment? Think about why. What reasons cause you to believe as you do?

Vocabulary

inalienable (par. 1)	depraved (par. 7)	deterrence (par. 9)
conscientiously (par. 4)	salutary (par. 8)	retribution (par. 9)
heinous (par. 5)	inherent (par. 8)	aggregate (par. 10)
plausible (par. 6)		

1   Many people believe that, as the Declaration of Independence affirms, all human beings are born with an inalienable right to life. Presumably, the reason, or at least one of the reasons, that murder is wrong is that it is a violation of the victim's right to life. But what of the criminal's right to life? In most societies throughout history, the punishment for murder has been execution. If the murderer is a human being, and surely he is, and if his right to life is inalienable, as human rights are usually taken to be, then the murderer has a right to life that he has not forfeited by his criminal act. It would appear that capital punishment is as much a violation of the fundamental human right to life as murder itself. It seems to follow that the execution of a condemned criminal is always wrong. This raises the question of whether there are any circumstances that morally justify capital punishment.

2   This question is an issue of lively debate these days. Great Britain abolished the death penalty in 1969 for all crimes except wartime offenses such as treason or spying, but with the increase in crimes of violence, there has been a rising demand for the restoration of capital punishment for crimes such as the murder of a policeman or a child. In *Furman v. Georgia* (1972), the United States Supreme Court declared unconstitutional any statute imposing capital punishment at the discretion of the judge or jury, but it left undecided the constitutionality of the death penalty itself. As a result, many

states have since then enacted new statutes making the imposition of the death penalty mandatory in the case of certain crimes such as first-degree murder or kidnapping. The morality and effectiveness of such statutes continues to be debated in Congress and in the state legislatures.

Defining the Problem

3   Let us try to define this specific moral problem more precisely. The expression "capital punishment" is ambiguous. It often refers to a certain kind of social institution. The institution of capital punishment is one pattern of punishment that forms part of the legal system in many, but not all, societies. It involves certain roles like those of the executioner and the criminal and certain rules such as the rule that only a person condemned to death by the courts is to be executed. One may well question the moral justifiability of this social institution, but this is not the question raised here. Instead, let us interpret the expression "capital punishment" as referring to a species of acts, acts of executing someone for conduct judged to be criminal.

4   The question is whether such acts are right or wrong; this is not to ask whether such acts are virtuous or wicked. Presumably the act of executing an innocent person is wrong, ought not to be done, even when there may be nothing wicked in the act of an executioner who conscientiously performs his painful duty in complete ignorance of any judicial error. Again, even if it is granted that a given act of executing an incurably vicious criminal is right, it would not follow that there is any moral goodness in the act if the executioner performs it in order to enjoy the suffering of the victim rather than from a sense of duty to society. To ask whether an act ought or ought not to be done is not to ask whether it is morally praiseworthy or blameworthy. It is the former, the question of rightness or wrongness, that is at issue here.

5   Finally, the question is whether capital punishment is ever right, whether there are any exceptional circumstances in which the act of executing a condemned criminal may be morally justifiable. No one could seriously maintain that capital punishment is always right, that condemned criminals should always be executed. An act of lynching performed by an enraged mob is a heinous wrong even

when the mob has condemned its victim with a mock trial. In a less spectacular way, it is morally wrong to take a criminal's life for any trivial crime like shoplifting or speeding on the highway. The only serious alternatives are that it is always wrong to execute a condemned criminal, no matter how great his crime, and that, in a few cases, it is right to take a criminal's life for conduct judged to be very, very wrong. Hence, the question worth discussing is "Is capital punishment ever right?"

Arguments for Capital Punishment

6   The classical and contemporary literature on the subject of capital punishment provides several very plausible arguments designed to prove that the act of executing a person for conduct judged to be criminal is sometimes right.

Prevention

7   Capital punishment is sometimes morally justified as a means of preventing the criminal from committing additional crimes. By his past action the criminal has shown himself to be wicked and dangerous. Anyone depraved enough to murder or rape once is very likely to act in socially harmful ways again. The only sure way to prevent such a person from going on to murder or rape in the future is to execute him. Imprisonment is a far less effective means of protecting society from such dangerous criminals. Most prisoners are freed after a time—often having become more dangerous than when they entered prison—by parole, pardon or the expiration of their sentences. In any case, escape is always possible. And even within the confines of prison, a condemned criminal may murder or rape a guard, a fellow inmate or a visitor. Executing a condemned criminal is the only sure way to prevent him from committing additional acts of crime. Since it is only right to protect the innocent members of society from the most serious crimes, capital punishment is sometimes right.

Deterrence

8   Not only does capital punishment prevent the criminal himself

from doing further harm to society, it also deters others from doing similar acts. Most people are tempted from time to time to do illegal and immoral acts; but the normal person is usually inhibited by conscience, or by fear of public condemnation, from serious wrongdoing. Some people, alas, require a stronger motive to overcome their criminal inclinations, and only the strongest threats of punishment can hold in check the strong emotions that cause the greatest crimes. Since almost everyone is terrified of death, capital punishment provides this salutary motive. The execution of one condemned criminal serves as an example to others of what may well befall them if they yield to their criminal impulses. Although very few potential criminals have personally witnessed executions, and fewer still have suffered them, the publicity given to the hanging or electrocution of condemned murderers and kidnappers has made almost everyone aware that the threat of the death penalty is no empty gesture. This knowledge, stimulating the deep and powerful fear of death inherent in human nature, deters potential criminals from the socially harmful acts they would otherwise commit. Since capital punishment sometimes deters potential criminals from doing socially harmful acts, and since it is right to protect society from seriously harmful acts, capital punishment is sometimes right.

Retribution

9   While the arguments from prevention and deterrence look to the future and attempt to justify capital punishment by an appeal to the future harm it will avoid, the argument from retribution looks to the past and tries to justify capital punishment as the right response to the wrong that has been done. Granted that society would be unjustified in taking a person's life in punishment for any trivial crime, capital punishment is just retribution for the greatest crimes. If one person has killed another, it is only fair that he give his own life in return. Kidnapping and rape are also so very wrong that the person who commits these acts deserves the greatest penalty, death. Justice demands that each individual be treated by others and by society as he deserves. The person who does good acts ought to be rewarded with good, and the person who does evil ought to suffer evil—each in proportion to the good or evil done. The conception of justice implicit in this argument has traditionally been illustrated by

the figure of a blindfolded woman holding a set of balance scales. The woman is blindfolded so that she cannot recognize her friends and enemies and award the former more good and the latter more evil than they deserve. The balance scales symbolizes the element of retribution, the notion that good or evil are to be awarded in return for good or evil done. The total conception is that justice demands that each person receive what is due to him, that he receive an amount of good or evil that is equal to the good or evil he has done. Applied to punishment, this means that the punishment should fit the crime, that the evil inflicted upon the condemned criminal should be in proportion to the degree of harm he has done. Since the only penalty bad enough to equal the greatest crimes is death, and since justice requires that the criminal receive just retribution for his past misdeeds, and since it is right to do what justice requires, capital punishment is sometimes right.

Self-Defense

[10]   Capital punishment is sometimes right because it is sometimes an exercise of society's right to self-defense. Although it is generally wrong for one human being to take the life of another, there are exceptional cases where this is morally justified. A person has a right to kill his attacker if this is necessary to preserve his life or limb. Society, like the individual, has the right to preserve itself when its very existence is threatened. Now a murderer attacks, not only his individual victim, but society itself. Since a society is constituted by an aggregate of individuals, to kill one or more individuals is already to begin to exterminate the society. Moreover, certain laws, such as the law prohibiting murder, are necessary if any collection of individuals are to live together in organized society. Hence, to break those laws that alone make the existence of society possible is to threaten that society with death. Capital punishment is sometimes right because it is right for society to exercise its right to self-defense, and in extreme cases capital punishment does defend the society from the attacks of a criminal that threatens its very existence.

31

Fulfilling a Duty

[11]   Executing a condemned criminal is sometimes right because it fulfills the duty of the executioner. Each of us plays many roles in society. I, for example, am a husband, a father, a citizen and a professor. Each social role brings with it certain duties. As a husband, my duties are at least to support my wife financially, to share certain household responsibilities, and to care for my wife in sickness and in health. To accept the position of professor in a university is to accept the duties of preparing lectures, grading tests and papers, holding regular office hours when students come for help in their studies, and doing original research as well. Similarly, the social role of public executioner brings with it certain duties, the chief of which is executing those condemned to death by the courts. No doubt it would be morally wrong for you or me to take the life of the criminal, no matter how guilty he might be. But it is right for the executioner to perform the act of capital punishment because he is acting in fulfillment of his duty as public executioner, and it is right to fulfill the duties of one's social role.

[12]   These are five arguments for capital punishment. It prevents the criminal from doing additional evil acts. It deters others from committing serious crimes. It is just retribution for the great wrong the criminal has done. It is society's act of killing in self-defense. And it fulfills the chief duty of the executioner. It is worth remembering that none of these arguments pretends to prove that all acts of capital punishment are right; each is intended to show only that it is sometimes right to execute a condemned criminal.

Thinking and Responding to the Reading

1. What is Wellman's argument (claim, conclusion)? Is it descriptive or prescriptive?
2. In Cornell-Note form, list the five reasons he gives and offer major supporting evidence for each.
3. Is this essay inductive or deductive? Using the definitions of the terms, explain your answer.

4. What are Wellman's values? What inference can you make from Wellman's values?
5. Does Wellman offer a valid argument based on the test for soundness and validity?

Chainsaws and Chigger Bites

Marie Cobb

Activate Your Schema: Think of a time when you had to learn how to use a tool for the first time. What senses did you rely on? What were you attempting to achieve? Did you get any help?

Vocabulary

crosscut (par. 1)	relative (par. 12)	chigger (par. 21)
apprehensive (par. 11)	acquisition (par. 20)	

1   As I was growing up in Tennessee, the only experience I had with tools was on my grandparents' farm with my grandfather and uncles who thought girls—and especially blind girls—had no business using such things. The most I ever was allowed to do was pull one end of a crosscut saw or screw a black walnut in a vice to hold it while I cracked it with a hammer. Power tools of any kind were certainly off limits.

2   Bright and early one hot summer morning five or six years ago the telephone rang and I heard my dad ask in a voice that sounded very chipper, "Are you alive?"

3   I did not want to admit that I was sitting in my bed drinking my first cup of tea and reading a good book. I answered, "Certainly."

4   "What are you doing today?" he asked.

5   "Oh, I don't know. What do you want me to do?" I asked with no idea of what the answer might be, since with Dad one never knew.

6   "If you haven't had breakfast yet, why don't you come over, and we'll have a bite and talk about what you might do this morning."

7   I said I would come in about half an hour after I had taken a shower and dressed.

8   "You don't need to do all that. Just put on some old

clothes and come on now. I'm hungry. The gate is open." And he hung up the phone.

9   While we were having fruit and cereal, you can imagine my delight when he asked me in a very casual manner if I had ever learned how to use a chainsaw. Of course I had to admit that somehow I never had but that I would like to since I shared his love of gadgets. "Well, as soon as we're finished here, I'll teach you. A girl ought to know how to use a chainsaw," he said.

10   When we went out to the wood garage, he got out a contraption that looked like a vice on legs and took a tree branch about four feet long and about the size of my forearm and secured it with the clamps. He showed me the controls and how to place the blade exactly on the spot I wanted to cut before pushing the power switch. Then, he told me to put my hands on top of his while he made the first cut.

11   As those of you who are familiar with my father know, he was blind from birth, but what you may not know is so was I. Therefore, I was just a wee bit apprehensive since chainsaws are so noisy and neither of us could see what we were doing, although I knew he wouldn't have been showing me how to do something that wasn't safe, and besides, I didn't want him to think I was a coward.

12   After he had done a couple of pieces, it was my turn, and I discovered that it was great fun to zip through pieces of wood with such relative ease. When he was sure I could handle the saw competently, he said, "Now over here I have a big stack of these limbs you can cut up for me to burn in my fireplace."

13   In a couple of hours I had what I thought was a very respectable pile of wood, of which I was quite proud.

14   Getting the wood cut up was a good and productive thing to do, but the most important thing that happened that day was that I gained a little more confidence in my ability to use power tools.

15   On the following Saturday I happened to mention to Dad that I knew where there was a lot more wood about the size of the limbs we had cut earlier in the week. He wanted to know where they were, and I told him in the woods a block or so from his house.

16   "Show me," he said, and off we went.

17   By the middle of the afternoon when I was tired and bathed in perspiration, I wasn't so sure it had been such a good idea to tell him about the dead branches in the woods.

¹⁸ I had dragged many long pieces of wood back to his driveway, and some of them were too long and heavy for me to handle by myself. Of course Dad had a solution for that problem.

¹⁹ "Take this little handsaw over and cut the long ones into more manageable pieces," he said. I said somewhat sheepishly that I had never been able to use one of those successfully. "Nonsense. I know exactly what you are doing wrong," he said. Of course he really did. I had always put too much pressure on the saw instead of letting the blade just ride along the top of the wood until it caught on its own.

²⁰ After several more trips to the woods I finished cutting the wood. Later that night I discovered that I had made another acquisition that day besides learning to use a saw.

²¹ I woke up itching in several places, and realized from past experiences that I was covered with chigger bites. It was definitely time to get out the nail polish to seal off the little holes they had made in my skin for breathing purposes.

²² Using a hand saw proved to be much harder work than using an electric chainsaw, but I was glad to have the knowledge and to have learned a new skill. Sometimes it is necessary to remind myself that blindness is not the reason why I can't or don't do certain things. It is simply that I haven't tried yet, and there is the big difference.

²³ We are all so thoroughly brainwashed concerning the so-called limitations of blindness that we have to guard against not allowing ourselves the freedom to accept all the exciting challenges the world has to offer.

Thinking and Responding to the Reading

1. List the steps Cobb's father uses to guide her in her various tasks.
2. Complete the following outline based on Cobb's essay.
   I. Main problem in question form
   II. Background information
      a. Relevant facts
      b. Significant feelings
      c. Problems encountered along the way
   III. Solution in statement form

3. Did Cobb use creative thinking, critical thinking or both thinking processes to solve her problems? How do you know this?

Childhood Obesity Report, 2011

United States Centers for Disease Control

Activate Your Schema: Think about the foods you typically eat in a day. Do you think you eat a healthful and nutritious diet?

Vocabulary

obesity (par. 1)	nutrition (par. 2)	nutrients (par. 4)
epidemic (par. 1)	behavioral (par. 3)	sedentary (par. 5)
sectors (par. 1)	indicators (par. 3)	domains (par. 6)
prevalence (par. 2)		

1   The current childhood obesity epidemic is the result of many factors and may not be resolved by any single action. Rather, resolution of the childhood obesity epidemic will require concerted action across many sectors and settings such as child- care facilities, communities, and schools.

2   The environments to which children are exposed in their daily lives—schools, child care facilities, and their communities—can influence the healthfulness of their diets. With the high prevalence of childhood obesity in the U.S., supporting healthy food environments is a key strategy to reach the public health goals of reducing childhood obesity and improving nutrition. On a state and local level, parents, school and child-care staff, health professionals, state officials, and community members play a role in supporting policy and environmental change to ensure children and their families can choose more healthful foods.

Behavioral Indicators

3   In this report, four behavioral indicators are reported: percentage of high school students who drank =1 sugar-sweetened soda per day, percentage of high school students who watched television =3 hours per day, percentage of children ages 6-17 with television in their bedroom, and percentage of children ages 12-17 who do not eat meals with their families most days of the week.

[4]   Sugar drinks are the largest source of added sugar and an important contributor of calories in the diets of children in the United States. Adolescent males consume, on average, around 300 calories from sugar drinks each day. High consumption of sugar drinks, which have few, if any, nutrients, has been associated with obesity.

[5]   Parents can positively impact children's sedentary activity, snacking, and exposure to advertising of unhealthy foods through rules related to TV viewing. One approach that parents can use to encourage healthy lifestyles for children at home is to not put televisions in children's bedrooms. The presence of a television in a child's bedroom has been associated with increased time spent watching television and increased prevalence of obesity. The link to obesity may occur through multiple mechanisms including displacement of physical activity, increased sugar drink intake while viewing, or through greater exposure to television advertising of unhealthy foods, which may affect food choices. The American Academy of Pediatrics (AAP) recommends that children should not have a television in their bedroom.

[6]   Parents have tremendous influence on children's food behaviors. Eating meals together as a family is associated with positive effects on children across many domains of life, including the development of healthy eating behaviors and the maintenance of a healthy weight status. Foods prepared and consumed at home may also be more nutritious than foods prepared away from home.

The School Food Environment

[7]   The Institute of Medicine recommends that the sale of competitive foods in schools (food sold outside the USDA reimbursable school meal programs such as in vending machines, school stores, snack bars) be limited. Schools are uniquely positioned to facilitate and reinforce healthful eating behaviors by eliminating sugar drinks and high-energy-density foods (foods high in calories for their volume) from the selection of foods offered on the school campus.

[8]   **Percentage of middle and high schools that offer sugar drinks as competitive foods.** Although sodas are prohibited in an increasing number of schools, other sugar drinks that may not be commonly perceived as sources of added sugar and excess calories may be available, such as sports drinks and fruit- flavored drinks that

are not 100% juice. Schools should consider adopting policies that limit access to all sugar drinks in vending machines and school stores.

[9] **Percentage of middle and high schools that offer less healthful foods as competitive foods.** Because human appetite and satiation depend more on the volume of food consumed than on caloric content of the food, reducing the consumption of energy-dense, low-nutrient foods has been identified as a strategy to prevent weight gain. Foods of lower energy density and higher nutrient content such as fruits and vegetables in their natural forms, nonfat/low-fat dairy products, and whole grain products are healthful alternatives to high energy density foods such as candy, cakes, salty fried snacks, and ice cream.

[10] **Percentage of middle and high schools that allow advertising of less healthful foods.** The Institute of Medicine has concluded that "food advertising to children affects their preferences, purchase behaviors, and consumption habits for different food and beverage categories, as well as for different product brands." In schools, advertising can take the form of posters and signage; logos or brand names on food and beverage coolers, cups, and plates or vending machines; food sales as fundraisers; corporate sponsorship of events; advertising in school publications; and corporate-sponsored classroom curricula and scholarships. Such advertising may impact children's ability to make healthy choices in their diets.

[11] Childhood and teen obesity levels can be attacked on several fronts. Children and teens should limit their consumption of added sugar, the leading source of which is sugar-sweetened drinks. Children and adolescents should not exceed the recommended limit for screen time of two hours a day for children two years and older. Other behavioral indicators include not placing televisions in children's bedrooms, and for children to have meals together with their family. Schools should emphasize foods of lower energy density and higher nutrients, and rethink the negative consequences of advertising of less healthful foods. Placing emphasis on these behavioral aspects in the home and at school will help in the fight against obesity.

Behavioral Indicators				
State	% HS Students Who Drank =1 Soda/Day	% HS Students Who Watched 3+ Hours of TV/Day	% Children Ages 6- 17 with TV in Bedroom	% Children Ages 12-17 Not Eating Family Meals Most Days of Week
U.S. Nat'l	29.2	32.8	50.2	30.7
Alabama	38.8	37.8	67.7	39.0
Alaska	20.1	24.8	33.0	28.7
Arizona	28.1	33.3	47.3	27.9
Arkansas	33.5	36.4	65.9	30.7
California			46.4	26.7
Colorado	24.6	25.1	36.6	23.9
Connecticut		30.2	42.9	32.6
Delaware	28.8	37.7	51.9	34.9
D.C.		58.8	35.7	
Florida	28.6	38.2	61.4	27.3
Georgia	29.7	39.2	56.1	31.0
Hawaii	20.8	30.1	39.3	25.0
Idaho	18.3	21.9	35.2	27.6
Illinois	31.1	35.7	50.9	34.9
Indiana	29.7	29.0	52.8	33.5
Iowa	43.9	31.7		
Kansas	30.7	28.3	43.1	32.7
Kentucky	35.7	28.8	62.4	32.1
Louisiana	36.6	40.3	70.6	37.7
Maine	25.4	39.9		30.7
Maryland	21.3	39.1	46.0	31.8
Massa-chusetts	21.0	30.4	36.3	30.0
Michigan	27.6	29.6	47.5	28.0
Minnesota			30.5	34.4
Mississippi	40.2	44.9	69.3	32.8
Missouri	31.5	32.4	52.5	33.2

Behavioral Indicators				
State	% HS Students Who Drank =1 Soda/Day	% HS Students Who Watched 3+ Hours of TV/Day	% Children Ages 6- 17 with TV in Bedroom	% Children Ages 12-17 Not Eating Family Meals Most Days of Week
Montana	25.7	23.7	36.3	26.3
Nebraska	40.5	31.7		
Nevada	22.1	35.1	59.1	28.0
New Hampshire	22.1	23.0	35.5	29.5
New Jersey	19.9	32.6	48.5	30.5
New Mexico	30.4	32.6	50.0	23.5
New York	24.5	32.7	48.9	33.2
North Carolina	32.5	36.2	58.2	28.3
North Dakota	26.3	25.6	43.1	27.7
Ohio	51.0	30.4		
Oklahoma	38.1	29.0	58.8	27.3
Oregon			41.6	27.5
Pennsyl-vania	25.7	30.8	50.9	33.7
Rhode Island	21.2	29.1	47.7	32.0
South Carolina	33.2	39.7	60.6	34.9
South Dakota	28.8	22.6	38.2	29.1
Tennessee	41.3	37.7	61.2	35.1
Texas	32.8	36.3	54.2	33.7
Utah	14.5	16.3	24.4	22.3
Vermont	22.9	31.0	25.9	
Virginia		47.6	33.3	
Washington		32.0	25.8	
West Va.	34.5	31.5	66.7	27.0
Wisconsin	23.1	23.1	40.4	33.3
Wyoming	27.0	22.0	41.5	26.6

42

Data Sources

Percentage of high school students who drank =1 sugar-sweetened soda per day. Available at http://www.cdc.gov/HealthyYouth/yrbs/index.htm

Percentage of high school students who watched television =3 hours per day. Available at http://www.cdc.gov/HealthyYouth/yrbs/index.htm

Percentage of children ages 6-17 years with television in bedroom. Available at: http://nschdata.org/Content/Guide2007.aspx.

Percentage of children ages 12-17 who do not eat with family most days of the week. Available at: http://nschdata.org/Content/Guide2007.aspx.

Thinking and Responding to the Reading

1. What is the overall argument of the essay? Although it has both prescriptive and descriptive arguments, identify the predominant type of argument and explain your answer.
2. List the factors that increase childhood obesity; then list the corresponding recommendation to combat each factor.
3. What assumptions are made about the role of schools and families in combating childhood obesity? Identify the prescriptive and descriptive assumptions for each role.
4. What do you think is the connection between eating meals as a family and lowering obesity rates?
5. Do you think the government should regulate the types of foods that are allowed in schools? Grocery stores? Explain your position(s).

Cinderella

A Folktale of China

Activate Your Schema: Do you recall Disney's movie or book version of *Cinderella*? As you read this version of the story, think about how they are similar and different.

Vocabulary

quandary (par. 9)	console (par. 16)	entrails (par. 20)
consciousness (par. 14)	innumerable (par. 18)	

1   There were once two sisters. The elder was very beautiful, and everyone called her Beauty. But the younger had a face covered with pock marks, so that everyone called her Pock Face. She was the daughter of the second wife, and was so spoiled that she was a very unpleasant girl. Beauty's real mother had died when Beauty was very young. After her death she turned into a yellow cow and lived in the garden. Beauty adored the yellow cow, but it had a miserable existence because the stepmother treated it so badly.

2   One day the stepmother took the ugly daughter to the theater and left Beauty at home. Beauty wanted to accompany them, but the stepmother said, "I will take you tomorrow if you straighten the hemp in my room."

3   Beauty went off and sat down in front of the stack of hemp, but after a long time she had only divided half of it. Bursting into tears, she took it off to the yellow cow, who swallowed the whole mass and then spat it out again all neatly arranged piece by piece. Beauty dried her tears, and gave the hemp to her mother on her return home. "Mother, here is the hemp. I can go to the theater tomorrow, can't I?"

4   When the next day came, her stepmother again refused to take her, saying, "You can go when you have separated the sesame seeds from the beans."

5   The poor girl had to divide them seed by seed, until the exhausting task made her eyes ache. Again she went to the yellow cow, who said to her, "You stupid girl! You must separate them

44

with a fan." Now she understood, and the sesame and beans were soon divided. When she brought the seeds all nicely separated, her stepmother knew that she could no longer prevent her going to the theatre. However, she asked her, "How can a servant girl be so clever? Who helped you?"

6   Beauty had to admit that the yellow cow had advised her, which made the stepmother very angry. Therefore, without saying a word, she killed and ate the cow. Beauty had loved the cow so dearly that she could not eat its flesh. Instead, she put the bones in an earthenware pot and hid them in her bedroom.

7   Day after day, the stepmother would still not take Beauty to the theater. One evening, when the stepmother had gone to the theater with Pock Face, Beauty was so cross that she smashed everything in the house, including the earthenware pot containing the cow's bones. Whereupon there was a loud crackling sound, and a white horse, a new dress, and a pair of embroidered shoes came out. The sudden appearance of these things gave Beauty a terrible start, but she soon saw that they were real objects. Quickly pulling on the new dress and the shoes, she jumped on the horse and rode out of the gate.

8   While she was riding along, one of her shoes slipped off and fell into the ditch. She wanted to dismount and pick it up, but could not do so; at the same time, she did not want to leave it lying there.

9   She was in a real quandary, when a fishmonger appeared. "Brother fishmonger, please pick up my shoe," she said to him. He answered with a grin, "With great pleasure, if you will marry me." "Who could marry you?" she said crossly. "Fishmongers always stink." Seeing that he had no chance, the fishmonger went on his way.

10   Next, a clerk from a rice shop went by, and she said to him, "Brother rice broker, please give me my shoe." "Certainly, if you will marry me," said the young man. "Marry a rice broker! Their bodies are all covered with dust."

11   The rice broker departed, and soon an oil merchant came by, whom she also asked to pick up her shoe. "I will pick it up if you consent to marry me," he replied. "Who could want to

marry you?" Beauty said with a sigh. "Oil merchants are always so greasy."

12   Shortly a scholar came by, whom she also asked to pick up her shoe. The scholar turned to look at her, and then said, "I will do so at once if you promise to marry me." The scholar was very handsome, and so she nodded her head in agreement. He picked up the shoe and put it on her foot. Then he took her back to his house and made her his wife.

13   Three days later, Beauty went with her husband to pay the necessary respects to her parents. Her stepmother and sister had quite changed their manner, and treated them both in the most friendly and attentive fashion. In the evening they wanted to keep Beauty at home, and she, thinking they meant it kindly, agreed to stay and to follow her husband in a few days.

14   The next morning her sister took her by the hand and said to her with a laugh, "Sister, come and look into the well. We will see which of us is the most beautiful." Suspecting nothing, Beauty went to the well and leaned over to look down. At this moment her sister gave her a shove and pushed her into the well; then she quickly covered the well with a basket. Poor Beauty lost consciousness and was drowned.

15   After ten days the scholar began to wonder why his wife had still not returned. He sent a messenger to inquire, and the stepmother sent back a message that his wife was suffering from a bad attack of smallpox and would not be well enough to return for some time. The scholar believed this, and every day he sent salted eggs and other sickbed delicacies, all of which found their way into the stomach of the ugly sister.

16   After two months the stepmother was irritated by the continual messages from the scholar, and decided to deceive him by sending back her own daughter as his wife. The scholar was horrified when he saw Pock Face, and said, "Goodness! How changed you are! Surely you are not Beauty. My wife was never such a monster. Good Heavens!" Pock Face replied seriously, "If I am not Beauty, who do you think I am then? You know perfectly well I was very ill with smallpox, and now you want to disown me. I shall die! I shall die!" She began to howl. The tender-hearted scholar could not bear to see her weeping, and although he still had some doubts, he begged

her forgiveness and tried to console her. Gradually she stopped weeping.

17   Beauty, however, had been transformed into a sparrow, and she used to come and call out when Pock Face was combing her hair, "Comb once, peep; comb twice, peep; comb thrice, up to the spine of Pock Face." The wicked wife answered, "Comb once, comb twice, comb thrice, to the spine of Beauty." The scholar was very mystified by this conversation, and he said to the sparrow, "Why do you sing like that? Are you by any chance my wife? If you are, call three times, and I will put you in a golden cage and keep you as a pet." The sparrow called out three times, and the scholar brought a golden cage to keep it in.

18   The ugly sister was very angry when she saw that her husband was keeping the sparrow, and so she secretly killed it and threw it into the garden. It was at once transformed into a bamboo with many shoots. When Pock Face ate the bamboo shoots, an ulcer formed on her tongue, but the scholar found them excellent. The wicked woman became suspicious again, and had the bamboo cut down and made into a bed. When she lay on it, innumerable needles pricked her, but the scholar found it extremely comfortable. Again she became very cross and threw the bed away.

19   Next door to the scholar lived an old woman who sold money bags. One day on her way home she saw the bed and thought to herself, "No one has died here; why have they thrown the bed away? I shall take it." She took the bed into her house and had a very comfortable night.

20   The next day she saw that the food in the kitchen was already cooked. She ate it up, but naturally she felt a little nervous, not knowing who could have prepared it. For several days she found she could have dinner the moment she came home. Finally, being no longer able to contain her anxiety, she came back early one afternoon and went into the kitchen, where she saw a dark shadow washing rice. She ran up quickly and clasped the shadow round the waist. "Who are you?" she asked, "and why do you cook food for me?" The shadow replied, "I will tell you everything. I am the wife of your neighbor the scholar and am called Beauty. My sister threw me into the well; I was drowned, but my soul was not destroyed. Please give me a rice pot as head, a stick as hand, a dish cloth as entrails, and firehooks as feet, and then I can assume my former shape again."

21   The old woman gave her what she asked for, and in a moment
a beautiful girl appeared. The old woman was delighted at seeing
such a charming girl, and she questioned her very closely about who
she was and what had happened to her. She told the old woman
everything, and then said, "Old woman, I have a bag which you must
offer for sale outside the scholar's house. If he comes out, you must
sell it to him." And she gave her an embroidered bag.

22   The next day the old woman stood outside the scholar's house
and shouted that she had a bag for sale. Maddened by the noise, he
came out to ask what kind of bags she sold, and she showed him
Beauty's embroidered bag. "Where did you get this bag?" he asked,
"I once gave it to my wife." The old woman then told the whole
story to the scholar, who was overjoyed to hear that his wife was still
alive. He arranged everything with the old woman, put a red cloth
on the ground, and brought Beauty back to his house.

23   When Pock Face saw her sister return, she gave her no peace.
She began to grumble and say that the woman was only pretending
to be Beauty, and that actually she was a spirit. She wanted to have a
trial to see which was the genuine wife. Beauty, of course, knew that
she herself was the real bride. She said, "Good. We will have a test."
Pock Face suggested that they should walk on eggs, and whoever
broke the shells would be the loser. Although Pock Face broke all
the eggs, and Beauty none, Pock Face refused to admit her loss and
insisted on another trial.

24   This time they were to walk up a ladder made of knives.
Beauty went up and down first without receiving the tiniest scratch,
but before Pock Face had gone two steps her feet were cut to the
bone. Although she had lost again, she insisted on another test—that
of jumping into a cauldron of hot oil. She hoped that Beauty, who
would have to jump first, would be burned. Beauty, however, was
quite unharmed by the boiling oil, but the wicked sister jumped into
it and did not come up again.

25   Beauty put the roasted bones of the wicked sister into a box
and sent them over to her stepmother by a stuttering old servant
woman, who was told to say, "Your daughter's flesh." But the
stepmother loved carp and understood "carp flesh" instead of "your
daughter's flesh." She thought her daughter had sent her over some
carp, and opened the box in a state of great excitement; but when she

saw the charred bones of her daughter lying inside, she let out a piercing scream and fell down dead.

 Thinking and Responding to the Reading

1. Look up the definition of a folktale. How does this story fit the definition?
2. How do the names in this story reveal the personalities of the characters?
3. Compare and contrast this version of the Cinderella story to the one you know.
4. Describe each competition between the two sisters. Why do they compete to their deaths?
5. What is the theme or moral of this story?

Daddy Tucked the Blanket

Randall Williams

Activate Your Schema: How do you define a home? What is the difference between a home and a house? What are your expectations of a home?

Vocabulary

conscious (par. 3)   articulate (par. 7)   psyche (par. 20)
humiliating (par. 5)   futility (par. 13)   retrospect (par. 25)

1   About the time I turned sixteen, my folks began to wonder why I didn't stay home any more. I always had an excuse for them, but what I didn't say was that I had found my freedom and I was getting out.

2   I went through four years of high school in semi-rural Alabama and became active in clubs and sports; I made a lot of friends and became a regular guy, if you know what I mean. But one thing was irregular about me. I managed those four years without ever having a friend visit at my house.

3   I was ashamed of where I lived. I had been ashamed for as long as I had been conscious of class.

4   We had a big family. There were several of us sleeping in one room, but that's not so bad if you get along, and we always did. As you get older, though, it gets worse.

5   Being poor is a humiliating experience for a young person trying hard to be accepted. Even now—several years removed—it is hard to talk about it. And I resent the weakness of these words to make you feel what it was really like.

6   We lived in a lot of old houses. We moved a lot because we were always looking for something just a little better than what we had. You have to understand that my folks worked harder than most people. My mother was always at home, but for her that was a full-time job—and no fun, either. But my father worked his head off from the time I can remember in construction and shops. It was hard, physical work.

[7]   I tell you this to show that we weren't shiftless. No matter how much money Daddy made, we never made much progress up the social ladder. I got out thanks to a college scholarship and because I was a little more articulate than the average.

[8]   I have seen my Daddy wrap copper wire through the soles of his boots to keep them together in the wintertime. He couldn't buy new boots because he had used the money for food and shoes for us. We lived like hell, but we went to school well-clothed and with a full stomach.

[9]   It really is hell to live in a house that was in bad shape ten years before you moved in. And a big family puts a lot of wear and tear on a new house, too, so you can imagine how one goes downhill if it is teetering when you move in. But we lived in houses that were sweltering in summer and freezing in winter. I woke up every morning for a year and a half with plaster on my face where it had fallen out of the ceiling during the night.

[10]   This wasn't during the Depression; this was in the late 60's and early 70's.

[11]   When we boys got old enough to learn trades in school, we would try to fix up the old house we lived in. But have you ever tried to paint a wall that crumbled when the roller went across it? And bright paint emphasized the holes in the wall. You end up more frustrated than when you began, especially when you know that at best you might come up with only enough money to improve one of the six rooms in the house. And we might move out soon after, anyway.

[12]   The same goes for keeping a house like that clean. If you have a house full of kids and the house is deteriorating, you'll never keep it clean. Daddy used to yell at Mama about that, but she couldn't do anything. I think Daddy knew it inside, but he had to have an outlet for his rage somewhere, and at least yelling isn't as bad as hitting, which they never did to each other.

[13]   But if you have a kitchen which has no counter space and no hot water, you will have dirty dishes stacked up. That sounds like an excuse, but try it. You'll go mad from the sheer sense of futility. It's the same thing in a house with no closets. You can't keep clothes clean and rooms in order if they have to be stacked up with things.

[14]   Living in a bad house is generally worse on girls. For one

thing, they traditionally help their mother with the housework. We boys could get outside and work in the fields or cut wood or even play ball and forget about living conditions. The sky was still pretty.

15   But the girls got the pressure, and as they got older it became worse. Would they accept dates knowing they had to "receive" the young man in a dirty hallway with broken windows, peeling wallpaper and a cracked ceiling? You have to live it to understand it, but it creates a shame which drives the soul of a young person inward.

16   I'm thankful none of us ever blamed our parents for this because it could have crippled our relationships. As it worked out, only the relationship between our parents was damaged. And I think the harshness which they expressed to each other was just an outlet to get rid of their anger at the trap their lives were in. It ruined their marriage because they had no one to yell at but each other. I knew other families where the kids got the abuse, but we were too much loved for that.

17   Once I was about sixteen and Mama and Daddy had had a particularly violent argument about the washing machine, which had broken down. Daddy was on the back porch—that's where the only water faucet was—trying to fix it and Mama had a washtub out there, washing school clothes for the next day, and they were screaming at each other.

18   Later that night everyone was in bed and I heard Daddy get up from the couch where he was reading. I looked out from my bed across the hall and into their room. He was standing right over Mama and she was already asleep. He pulled the blanket up and tucked it around her shoulders and just stood there and tears were dropping off his cheeks and I thought I could faintly hear them splashing against the linoleum rug.

19   Now they're divorced.

20   I had courses in college where housing was discussed, but the sociologists never put enough emphasis on the impact living in substandard housing has on a person's psyche, especially children's.

21   Small children have a hard time understanding poverty. They want the same things children from more affluent families have. They want the same things they see advertised on television, and they don't understand why they can't have them.

52

22   Other children can be incredibly cruel. I was in elementary school in Georgia—and this is interesting because it is the only thing I remember about that particular school—when I was about eight or nine.

23   After Christmas vacation had ended, my teacher made each student describe all his or her Christmas presents. I became more and more uncomfortable as the privilege passed around the room toward me. Other children were reciting the names of the dolls they had been given, the kinds of bicycles and the grandeur of their games and toys. Some had lists which seemed to go on and on for hours.

24   It took me only a few seconds to tell the class what I had gotten for Christmas: a belt and a pair of gloves. And then I was laughed at—because I cried—by a roomful of children and a teacher. I never forgave them, and that night I made my mother cry when I told her about it.

25   In retrospect, I am grateful for that moment, but I remember wanting to die at the time.

Thinking and Responding to the Reading

1. What is the main point of this essay?
2. List the reasons Williams uses to support his main point.
3. Give three examples of observation. How do these observations advance his story?
4. What is Williams implying when he says, "I never forgave them, and that night I made my mother cry when I told her about it.... In retrospect, I am grateful for that moment, but I remember wanting to die at the time." (pars. 24-25).
5. Having read and thought about Williams' point, what connotative meaning would you now give for home?

The Dire Calamity and the Greater San Francisco Earthquake

Jack London

Activate Your Schema: What are the benefits versus the risks of building homes and businesses on land, like San Francisco, where it is known that natural disasters are likely to occur?

Vocabulary

dire (title)	entombed (par. 13)	profuse (par. 33)
calamity (title)	conflagration (par. 17)	adverse (par. 36)
seismic (par. 4)	cyclones (par. 28)	ascertained (par. 37)
metropolis (par. 4)	unabated (par. 30)	gratuitous (par. 33)
temblor (par. 7)	annals (par. 38)	fraught (par. 39)

1   Pioneer San Francisco received a rude awakening Wednesday morning, April 18, 1906.

2   The awful call came without warning, like a mysterious bolt of lightning, rushing through the upper strata of the earth, causing devastation, terror and death at the hour of thirteen minutes past five o'clock in the morning, when a large majority of the city's people were still asleep in their homes.

3   It seems as if all-wise Providence had chosen the most fortunate hour for the appalling catastrophe.

4   If the seismic disturbance had occurred in the daytime when the busy thoroughfares of the metropolis were lined with people, or in the evening when the theatres were crowded, there would have been a still more horrifying chapter in the world's history than the one which the city by the Golden Gate had just contributed.

5   Terrible as the distress and the calamity appear, the people of San Francisco and California have ample cause for genuine and deep-felt gratitude.

6   The earthquake shock did much damage.

[7] There is as little use in denying this fact as there is in exaggerating the results of the temblor.

[8] The first heavy shock, a few minutes after five in the morning, struck terror into the bravest and the coolest of the city's sleeping populace. In a few seconds the streets in the residence districts were lined with people who rushed out of their apartments and homes in night attire. Furniture, pianos, bookcases danced through the rooms as if possessed with demons; crockery and chinaware dashed out of their snug closets on the floors; chimneys toppled over and houses cracked, crushed and caved in.

[9] The lower portions of the city, and particularly where the buildings were resting on "filled" ground, seemed to have fared the worst.

[10] Most of the old buildings along Montgomery Street and east along the waterfront were badly cracked by the shock.

[11] The Valencia Hotel, near Eighteenth Street, caved in, and in the fall killed a number of lodgers and injured others.

[12] The large five-story Brunswick Hotel on Sixth and Howard streets, with its three hundred rooms which are all reported to have been occupied, collapsed to the ground.

[13] The Portland House, on Sixth Street, between Mission and Market, collapsed, and it is stated that about sixty persons were entombed among the crashing ruins. Their heart-rendering cries for help were heard a block away. A large number of these, however, were saved before the fire overtook them and taken to the emergency hospital established at the Mechanics' Pavilion.

[14] Nearly all the lodging-houses south of Market Street met the same fate.

[15] But although the damage from the earthquake was great, San Francisco would have recovered from the shock in a marvelously short space of time.

[16] It was not the earthquake, but the fire—the great terrible fire—that destroyed pioneer San Francisco.

[17] For three days and three nights that awful conflagration swept the stricken city, devouring half a century's fruition of human energy, skill and ingenuity.

[18] Fires broke out in a half dozen places shortly after the earthquake; and although our excellent fire-fighters responded promptly to the call of duty, they were greatly handicapped at the

very start by the lack of water, many of the mains having been broken by the temblor. Despite the firemen's heroic efforts the fire spread.

19   The old buildings south of Market and east of Seventh burned like so many boxes of matches, and the people fled before the ravaging elements to the nearest place of safety.

20   Men, women and children, most of them poorly clad, clutching a family picture, carrying some relic, a bundle of bed clothes, a grip or dragging a truck, hurried away from the scorching flames to what destinations they knew not.

21   They were motivated by but one thought—to get away from the terrible fire.

22   The gloomy tide of humanity rolled on, out through the Mission Road to the cemeteries, over the hills to Golden Gate Park and on to the beach. It was one mighty surging wave of human faces of living grief and throbbing despair.

23   Wednesday afternoon the fire broke out in Hayes Valley and swept on towards the St. Ignatious College, on Van Ness Avenue, totally destroying that noble structure.

24   The fire made short work of the Franklin Hotel; it blazed in a few minutes and fell into Market Street.

25   The Mechanics' Pavilion was an easy prey to the flames, but the sick and injured were rushed out to other improvised hospitals before the fire reached the pavilion.

26   East and west, north and south, the terrible conflagration ate its way.

27   On Wednesday night and Thursday morning the lower portion of Market Street, Chinatown and Nob Hill was one seething furnace.

28   Thousands of angry flames shot high into the sky, and the cracking timbers, the falling buildings and the terrific roar of the fire sounded like a dozen cyclones.

29   Thursday morning dawned on the dire calamity, but it brought additional terror to the stricken people. The fire was still raging worse than on Wednesday, and the black smoke hung over the doomed city like a shroud of death.

30   Thursday, Thursday night, Friday, Friday night and

Saturday the all-destructive fire continued its work of devastation unabated.

[31]   It was a panorama that people who saw it will never forget and never wish to see again, but through it all for three days and three nights the brave fire laddies fought the merciless element. Many of them dropped utterly exhausted at their post of duty, which was quickly taken up by one of their comrades. They stood in the smoke of the roaring furnaces to fight the flames, and cases are on record where police officers and volunteer firemen had to continually apply a stream of water on the regular firemen on duty to keep them from being burned or scorched.

[32]   Dynamiting of buildings was resorted to in an attempt to confine the fire, but the flames were no sooner subdued in one place than they broke out in another.

[33]   As is usual in all cases of extraordinary emergency, those who knew it all were profuse in their gratuitous advice of how things ought to be done, and the great San Francisco fire produced a few fire experts who were brim full of good ideas and wonderful theories, but they all kept a very safe distance from the fire.

[34]   Expressions were frequently heard from all sides to the effect that if the late Chief Sullivan had been well and alive, the fire would have been confined within a very limited area. No doubt there was considerable truth in these statements. Firefighting was the chosen profession of the late chief, and he had made a life study of the conditions presented by a big fire in San Francisco. In fact, he had often stated that San Francisco could not always escape a big conflagration, and he predicted on more than one occasion the great fire with its causes and terrible results which we have just passed through, but which he was not permitted to combat.

[35]   Time and again had he asked the ex-Board of Supervisors to provide an adequate water supply for the protection of the city against the fire, and as often did he ask in vain.

[36]   But regardless of the various and adverse comments both during the progress of the fire and afterward, the fact remains that every member of the San Francisco Fire Department battled for days and nights with the raging elements as men never fought

before. They were also ably assisted by the police department and the federal troops.

[37] It is stated that the edge of the fire limit is over twenty-nine miles long and the burnt area is composed as being over eight square miles. The property loss is variously estimated between $200,000,000 and $400,000,000. The exact loss of life has not yet, and never will be ascertained, but Coroner Walsh estimates it not less than fifteen hundred.

[38] Compared with the Chicago fire in 1871, the burned district in San Francisco is six times the size of the one laid bare in Chicago, and the property loss and loss of life comes very nearly in the same proportion. The dire calamity is the greatest and most distressing event of its kind not only in the history of our country, but within the annals of the world.

[39] Terrible as the disaster still appears before our eyes, it has already been fraught with many and wonderful blessings, and San Francisco's sad misfortune will in time prove to have been her best fortune.

 Thinking and Responding to the Reading

1. Paraphrase what happened in San Francisco in 1906.
2. What was the primary reason for the great conflagration?
3. What do we learn about Chief Sullivan? How does he compare with the fire chiefs who were present during the fire? What is London implying about leadership?
4. What are the "many blessings" and "her best fortune" that have come out of the calamity?
5. Have you ever lived through or read about others who lived through a natural disaster? What can you conclude about nature's power?
6. Compare this natural disaster to what is predicted in the article "Global Climate Change Impacts in the United States."

The Discus Thrower

Dr. Richard Selzer

Activate Your Schema: Have you ever had to care for someone who was "difficult" or have you ever been in a situation where you had no control? How did you feel and respond?

Vocabulary

furtive (par. 1)	repose (par. 2)	stolid (par. 20)
vigor (par. 2)	mute (par. 3)	inert (par. 20)
vile (par. 2)	caches (par. 4)	athwart (par. 20)

1   I spy on my patients. Ought not a doctor to observe his patients by any means and from any stance, that he might the more fully assemble evidence? So I stand in the doorways of hospital rooms and gaze. Oh, it is not all that furtive an act. Those in bed need only to look up to discover me. But they never do.

2   From the doorway of Room 542 the man in the bed seems deeply tanned. Blue eyes and close-cropped white hair give him the appearance of vigor and good health. But I know that his skin is not brown from the sun. It is rusted, rather, in the last stage of containing the vile repose within. And the blue eyes are frosted, looking inward like the windows of a snowbound cottage. This man is blind. This man is also legless—the right leg missing from mid-thigh down, the left from just below the knee, giving him the facsimile of a great tree.

3   Propped on pillows, he cups his right thigh in both hands. Now and then he shakes his head as though acknowledging the intensity of his suffering. In all of this he makes no sound. Is he mute as well as blind?

4   The room in which he dwells is empty of all possessions—no get-well cards, small, private caches of food, day-old flowers, slippers, all the usual kickshaws of the sickroom. There is only the bed, a chair, a nightstand, and a tray on wheels that can be swung across his lap for meals.

5   "What time is it?" he asks.

6   "Three o'clock."

7   "Morning or afternoon?"

8   "Afternoon."

9   He is silent. There is nothing else he wants to know.

10   "How are you?" I say.

11   "Who is it?" he asks.

12   "It's the doctor. How do you feel?"

13   He does not answer right away.

14   "Feel?" he says.

15   "I hope you feel better." I say.

16   I press the button at the side of the bed.

17   "Down you go," I say.

18   "Yes, down," he says.

19   He falls back upon the bed awkwardly. His stumps, unweighted by legs and feet, rise in the air, presenting themselves. I unwrap the bandages from the stumps, and begin to cut away the black scabs and the dead, glazed fat with scissors and forceps. A shard of white bone comes loose. I pick it away. I wash the wounds with disinfectant and redress the stumps. All this while, he does not speak. What is he thinking behind those lids that do not blink? Is he remembering a time when he was whole? Does he dream of feet? Of when his body was not a rotting log?

20   He lies stolid and inert. In spite of everything, he remains impressive, as though he were a sailor standing athwart a slanting deck.

21   "Anything more I can do for you?" I ask.

22   For a long moment he is silent.

23   "Yes," he says at last and without the least irony. "You can bring me a pair of shoes."

24   In the corridor, the head nurse is waiting for me.

25   "We have to do something about him," she says. "Every morning he orders scrambled eggs for breakfast, and, instead of eating them, he picks up the plate and throws it against the wall."

26   "Throws his plate?"

27   "Nasty. That's what he is. No wonder his family doesn't come to visit. They probably can't stand him any more than we can."

28   She is waiting for me to do something.

29   "Well?"

30   "We'll see," I say.

31   The next morning I am waiting in the corridor when the kitchen delivers his breakfast. I watch the aide place the tray on the

60

stand and swing it across his lap. She presses the button to raise the head of the bed. Then he leaves.

32   In time the man reaches to find the rim of the tray, then on to find the dome of the covered dish. He lifts off the cover and places it on the stand. He fingers across the plate until he probes the eggs. He lifts the plate in both hands, sets it on the palm of his right hand, centers it, balances it. He hefts it up and down slightly, getting the feel of it. Abruptly, he draws back his right arm as far as he can.

33   There is the crack of the plate breaking against the wall at the foot of his bed and small wet sound of the scrambled eggs dropping to the floor.

34   And then he laughs. It is a sound you have never heard. It is something new under the sun. It could cure cancer.

35   Out of the corridor, the eyes of the head nurse narrow.

36   "Laughed, did he?"

37   She writes something down on her clipboard.

38   A second aide arrives, brings a second breakfast tray, puts it on the night-stand, out of his reach. She looks over at me shaking her head and making her mouth go. I see that we are to be accomplices.

39   "I've got to feed you," she says to the man.

40   "Oh, no you don't," the man says.

41   "Oh, yes I do," the aide says, "after the way you just did. Nurse says so."

42   "Get me my shoes," the man says.

43   "Here's oatmeal," the aide says. "Open." And she touches the spoon to his lower lip.

44   "I ordered scrambled eggs," says the man.

45   "That's right," the aide says.

46   I step forward.

47   "Is there anything I can do?" I say.

48   "Who are you?" the man asks.

49   In the evening I go once more to that ward to make my rounds. The head nurse reports to me that Room 542 is deceased. She has discovered this quite by accident, she says. No, there had been no sound. Nothing. It's a blessing, she says.

50   I go into his room, a spy looking for secrets. He is still there in his bed. His face is relaxed, grave, dignified. After a while, I turn to leave. My gaze sweeps the wall at the foot of the bed, and I see the place where

it has been repeatedly washed, where the wall looks very clean and very white.

 Thinking and Responding to the Reading

1. In the first line, Selzer, the doctor who is narrating this memoir, describes himself as a "spy." Explain why he says this.
2. What is the main idea? Is it stated or implied?
3. Why do you think the patient throws the scrambled eggs on the wall? Why are the nurse and the nurse's aide upset by his behavior?
4. Selzer uses much figurative language to describe the patient. List three examples and explain each. What do they have in common? Think about what overall image or feeling Selzer is conveying.
5. What are the values the caregivers have towards their dying patient? In this essay, do the all the caregivers have the same values?
6. What are your cultural or religious views on death and dying? What are some other cultures' views? How do you think these views have changed since modern science has enabled doctors to prolong life?

A Fable for Tomorrow

Rachel Carson

Activate Your Schema: Think about a time when you used chemicals to try to influence nature. Do we now have "safe" chemicals to be used on crops and lawns, or ponds and lakes? Are alternative methods being sought or practiced?

Vocabulary

harmony (par. 1)	stricken (par. 3)	counterparts (par. 9)
blight (par. 3)	moribund (par. 4)	specter (par. 9)
maladies (par. 3)	withered (par. 6)	stark (par. 9)

1   There was once a town in the heart of America where all life seemed to live in harmony with its surrounds. The town lay in the midst of a checkerboard of prosperous farms, with fields of rain and hillsides of orchards where, in spring, white clouds of bloom drifted above the green fields. In autumn, oak and maple and birch set up a blaze of color that flamed and flickered across a backdrop of pines. Then foxes barked in the hills and deer silently crossed the fields, half hidden in the mists of the fall mornings.

2   Along the roads, laurel, viburnum and alder, great ferns and wildflowers delighted the traveler's eye through much of the year. Even in winter the roadsides were places of beauty, where countless birds came to feed on the berries and on the seed heads of the dried weeds rising above the snow. The countryside was, in fact, famous for the abundance and variety of its bird life, and when the flood of migrants was pouring through in spring and fall, people traveled from great distances to observe them. Others came to fish the streams, which flowed clear and cold out of the hills and contained shady pools where trout lay. So it had been from the days many years ago when the first settlers raised their houses, sank their wells, and built their barns.

3   Then a strange blight crept over the area and everything began to change. Some evil spell had settled on the community: mysterious maladies swept the flock of chickens; the cattle and the sheep

sickened and died. Everywhere was a shadow of death. The farmers spoke of much illness among their families. In the town the doctors had become more and more puzzled by new kinds of sickness appearing among their patients. There had been several sudden and unexplained deaths not only among adults but even among children, who would be stricken suddenly while at play and die within a few hours.

4   There was a strange stillness. The birds, for example—where had they gone? Many people spoke of them, puzzled and disturbed. The feeding stations in the backyards were deserted. The few birds seen anywhere were moribund; they trembled violently and could not fly. It was a spring without voices. On the mornings that had once throbbed with the dawn chorus of robins, catbirds, doves, jays, wrens, and scores of other bird voices there was now no sound; only silence lay over the fields and woods and marsh.

5   On the farms the hens brooded, but no chicks hatched. The farmers complained that they were unable to raise any pigs—the litters were small and the young survived only a few days. The apple trees were coming into bloom but no bees droned among the blossoms, so there was no pollination and there would be no fruit.

6   The roadsides, once so attractive, were now lined with browned and withered vegetation as though swept by fire. These, too, were silent, deserted by all living things. Even the streams were now lifeless. Anglers no longer visited them, for all the fish had died.

7   In the gutters under the eaves and between the shingles of the roofs, a white granular powder still showed a few patches; some weeks before it had fallen like snow upon the roofs and the lawns, the fields and the streams.

8   No witchcraft, no enemy action had silenced the rebirth of new life in this stricken world. The people had done it themselves.

9   This town does not actually exist, but it might easily have a thousand counterparts in America or elsewhere in the world. I know of no community that has experienced all the misfortunes I describe. Yet every one of these disasters has actually happened somewhere, and many real communities have already suffered a substantial number of them. A grim specter has crept upon us almost unnoticed, and this imagined tragedy may easily become a stark reality we all shall know.

Thinking and Responding to the Reading

1. What is a fable? Why does Carson title the essay "A Fable for Tomorrow"?
2. What is Carson's main point?
3. Carson uses cause and effect as a way of making her point. Compose a list of the effects of the "evil spell [that] had settled on the community."
4. Although Carson doesn't tell the readers what "strange blight crept over the area," she implies it. What do you think caused the change? What evidence makes you think this?
5. This essay is full of description. Pick three descriptive passages that you think are particularly effective. Paraphrase each one.

Forgiveness

Mykel C. Johnson

Activate Your Schema: Have you needed to ask forgiveness of someone or to forgive someone? Are there any circumstances that are not forgivable?

Vocabulary

foibles (par. 2)	atonement (par. 13)	redress (par. 18)
riled (par. 2)	apartheid (par. 16)	askew (par. 18)
sanctity (par. 5)	amnesty (par. 16)	atrocity (par. 20)
reconciliation (par. 6)	retributive (par. 18)	

1   Conflict is all around us. It is as local as a morning person and a night person trying to live in the same house. It is as world-shaking as the struggle between Israelis and Palestinians trying to share the same piece of land in the Middle East. Forgiveness is one of the tools we have for making peace.

2   Forgiveness is a form of love. It has its roots in a belief that persons are connected. When we care about cultivating and nurturing those bonds, we are more gentle with the foibles and limitations of others. We hold in our hearts a cooperative spirit. At the opposite extreme is to see others as separate and apart. Then it is easy for them to become competitors or enemies, to be a source of irritation. Driving a car in Boston was often an experience of such a disconnected perspective. With people yelling and honking and jockeying for position, I would start to feel tense and riled up, ready to snap at the next driver who slowed down to turn left. No wonder it explodes into the violence now identified as road rage. Forgiveness begins in small compassions, in overlooking the imperfections of others, to focus on their essential okay-ness: their sacredness.

3   Unitarian Universalists have always been liberal in our belief in the essential goodness of people and generous in our bestowal of forgiveness. There was a comic expression of this benevolence in a newspaper cartoon, Doug Marlett's "Kudzu." The first frame is a

picture of the Holy Roller preacher at bat in the interfaith baseball game. The umpire calls out, "Strike Three." In the next frames, the preacher is still at bat, as the ump shouts, "Strike Four, Strike Five." The preacher finally comments: "Unitarians—ya gotta love 'em."

[4] It was the Universalists who imagined a God so full of love that he would ultimately forgive everyone. In a time when most believed in divine judgment and eternal punishment, the Universalists declared that all would be restored: everyone would go to heaven. God was too loving to send any of his children to hell.

[5] For me, growing up in a Catholic environment, forgiveness was associated with great holiness. We learned the story of Saint Maria Goretti, a twelve-year-old Italian girl who was stabbed to death when she refused the sexual advances of a young man in her neighborhood. Part of the evidence of her sanctity was that on her deathbed she forgave her murderer. In this, she was following the example of Jesus, who prayed for his executioners from the cross: "Father forgive them, for they know not what they do." Jesus had taught his disciples to pray, "Forgive us our trespasses, as we forgive those who trespass against us." And when asked how often one must forgive a wrongdoer who apologized, he answered, "Seventy times seven times."

[6] But forgiveness got more complicated for me when I learned about the problem of domestic violence. When battered women began to speak up and seek out shelter, one of the issues that emerged was that the cycle of battering included apology and regret. Women were being urged by their priests and pastors to forgive their battering husbands as part of their Christian duty. But after the apologies and tearful reconciliations, the cycle of control and violence would only get worse. Forgiveness was not helping. Leaving the abuser was often the only option for breaking the cycle. And so I began to try to understand the limits of forgiveness.

[7] Resolving conflict requires all of us to acknowledge and deal with aggression and abuse. Otherwise, we are leaving the vulnerable in danger. As liberals we don't like to talk about evil or sin. But to be peacemakers we must be able to recognize when a line has been crossed beyond human faults and limitations and into abusive behavior. We must know when to forgive, and when forgiveness would be a mask for fear or weakness. When facing aggression, we must have the strength to confront and contain.

[8]   The great teacher of non-violence, Mahatma Gandhi, said, "Forgiveness is a virtue of the brave. He alone who is strong enough to avenge a wrong knows how to love and forgive. There is no question of the mouse forgiving the cat. It is not forgiveness if the mouse allows itself to be torn to pieces by her."

[9]   Simon Wiesenthal was a Jewish prisoner in a concentration camp in Poland. All around him, Jews were being killed every day. One day, on a work detail at a nearby hospital, he was brought by a nurse to the bed of a dying Nazi soldier. Once they were alone, the soldier painfully told him a long story of how he had participated in the horrible killing of Jewish families. The families had been herded into a building, and the building was set on fire. When they began to jump out the windows, the soldiers were ordered to shoot them. This young Nazi soldier had shot a father and his small son.

[10]   He grabbed onto Simon's hand, full of remorse. "I know that what I have told you is terrible. In the long nights while I have been waiting for death, time and time again I have longed to talk about it to a Jew and beg forgiveness from him. I know that what I am asking is almost too much for you, but without your answer I cannot die in peace."

[11]   Simon chose to remain silent....

[12]   Afterward, he was haunted by the incident. If you were Simon, what would you have done? Should he have forgiven the Nazi soldier? He raised the question again and again during and after the war. Eventually he created a book, *The Sunflower: On the Possibilities and the Limits of Forgiveness,* from the story and the responses he received from others.

[13]   According to a Jewish understanding, reconciliation can only happen between the wrongdoer and the one who was wronged. *Teshuvah* is the practice of repentance and comes from the Hebrew word "to return." There are three steps to a complete *teshuvah.* First, one must ask forgiveness of the person you have wronged. Judaism believes that it is only through human interaction that the victim can best be healed and the wrongdoer most profoundly changed. Second, one turns to God to confess one's wrongs, expressing shame and regret for having committed this act, and resolving never to act that way again. Third, when confronted with the same situation one chooses not to repeat the act. Judaism also distinguishes between repentance and atonement. Atonement only

comes after one bears the consequences of one's acts. Only after bearing the consequences of a wrongful act is one restored to right relationship with God and one's fellow humans.

[14]   With this understanding of forgiveness, most Jews expressed the belief that Simon had no power to forgive the Nazi because he was not the person who had been killed. In fact, murder is an unforgivable sin because there is no opportunity for apology to the victim. Simon Wiesenthal survived the camps and went on to work for the prosecution of Nazi war criminals. This was his way of trying to bring about atonement.

[15]   My questions about forgiveness and reconciliation brought me to Martha Minow's book *Between Vengeance and Forgiveness: Facing History After Genocide and Mass Violence*. She addresses the question of how people can break the cycle of revenge. I was especially moved by her account of the work of the Truth and Reconciliation Commission in South Africa.

[16]   The Commission was created as part of the compromise that brought an end to apartheid. South Africans concluded that to achieve unity and morally acceptable reconciliation, it was necessary that the truth about gross violations of human rights be established by an official investigation. The price for achieving this full disclosure was to offer amnesty to perpetrators. It was a conditional amnesty: it was only available to those who personally applied for it, and who disclosed fully the facts of misdeeds that could be characterized as having a political objective.

[17]   The primary focus of the Commission was on hearing the testimony of victims. Pumla Gobodo-Madikizela, a psychologist serving on the human rights committee, reported that many victims conceive of justice in terms of revalidating oneself, and of affirming the sense that you're right, you were damaged, and it was wrong. The Commission offered such validation as it heard testimony from survivors and family members of those who were tortured and murdered.

[18]   For Archbishop Desmond Tutu, the convener of the Commission, forgiveness and reconciliation were an important part of the process. He said, "Retributive justice is largely Western. The African understanding is far more restorative—not so much to punish as to redress or restore a balance that has been knocked

askew. The justice we hope for is restorative of the dignity of the people."

[19]   What role did forgiveness play in the Truth and Reconciliation Commission? Forgiveness was a refusal by the victim to dehumanize the perpetrators as they had been dehumanized. Forgiveness was an act of personal power that put the perpetrator and victim back on an equal level. Forgiveness was a commitment to the future, which was rooted deeper than the betrayals of the past. It has been in the hope and exhilaration of being full participants in creating a new country, that many have found the strength to bear the painful process of examining the wounds of the past.

[20]   The essence of forgiveness is that it cannot be required. And yet, to witness forgiveness in the hearts of those who have faced atrocity renews our sense of hope and faith in humanity. In a great injury, something is broken, psychologically or spiritually. The break erodes our sense of living in a fair world; it corrupts our experience of our own worth, and fragments our control over our own lives and emotions. But deeper than that, it also fundamentally damages our faith in the worthiness of others. Forgiveness somehow absorbs those losses and transforms them. To witness great forgiveness is to renew our experience of the sacredness of all people.

 Thinking and Responding to the Reading

1. List the five cultural perspectives on forgiveness that Johnson describes.
2. Explain the process of *teshuvah* as discussed in paragraph 13.
3. Explain the African perspective on forgiveness as described in paragraph 18.

4. What role did the Truth and Reconciliation Commission play in helping both perpetrator and victim? Be sure to explain "equal level" as described in paragraph 19.
5. Paraphrase paragraph 20. Explain your own definition of forgiveness after thinking about this essay.

Get a Knife, Get a Dog, but Get Rid of Guns

Molly Ivins

Activate Your Schema: What is your position on gun use in the United States?

Vocabulary

ricochet (par. 3)	infringed (par. 4)	wreak (par. 7)
civil libertarian (par. 4)	perforating (par. 5)	psyches (par. 13)

1 Guns. Everywhere guns.

2 Let me start this discussion by pointing out that I am not anti-gun. I'm pro-knife. Consider the merits of the knife.

3 In the first place, you have to catch up with someone in order to stab him. A general substitution of knives for guns would promote physical fitness. We'd turn into a whole nation of great runners. Plus, knives don't ricochet. And people are seldom killed while cleaning their knives.

4 As a civil libertarian, I, of course, support the Second Amendment. And I believe it means exactly what it says: *A well-regulated militia being necessary to the security of a free state, the right of the people to keep and bear arms shall not be infringed.* Fourteen-year-old boys are not part of a well-regulated militia. Members of wacky religious cults are not part of a well-regulated militia. Permitting unregulated citizens to have guns is destroying the security of this free state.

5 I am intrigued by the arguments of those who claim to follow the judicial doctrine of original intent. How do they know it was the dearest wish of Thomas Jefferson's heart that teenage drug dealers should cruise the cities of this nation perforating their fellow citizens with assault rifles? Channeling?

6 There is more hooey spread about the Second Amendment. It says quite clearly that guns are for those who form part of a well-

regulated militia, that is, the armed forces, including the National Guard. Their reasons for keeping them away from everyone else get clearer by the day.

[7] The comparison most often used is that of the automobile, another lethal object that is regularly used to wreak great carnage. Obviously, this society is full of people who haven't enough common sense to use an automobile properly. But we haven't outlawed cars yet.

[8] We do, however, license them and their owners, restrict their use to presumably sane and sober adults, and keep track of who sells them to whom. At a minimum, we should do the same with guns.

[9] In truth, there is no rational argument for guns in this society. This is no longer a frontier nation in which people hunt their own food. It is a crowded, overwhelmingly urban country in which letting people have access to guns is a continuing disaster. Those who want guns—whether for target shooting, hunting, or potting rattlesnakes (get a hoe) should be subject to the same restrictions placed on gun owners in England, a nation in which liberty has survived nicely without an armed populace.

[10] The argument that "guns don't kill people" is patent nonsense. Anyone who has ever worked in a cop shop knows how many family arguments end in murder because there was a gun in the house. Did the gun kill someone? No. But if there had been no gun, no one would have died. At least not without a good foot race first. Guns do kill. Unlike cars, that is all they do.

[11] Michael Crichton makes an interesting argument about technology in his thriller *Jurassic Park*. He points out that power without discipline is making this society into a wreckage. By the time someone who studies the martial arts becomes a master— literally able to kill with bare hands—that person has also undergone years of training and discipline. But any fool can pick up a gun and kill with it.

[12] "A well-regulated militia" surely implies both long training and long discipline. That is the least, the very least, that should be required of those who are permitted to have guns, because a gun is literally the power to kill. For years I used to enjoy taunting my gun-nut friends about their psychosexual hang-ups—always in a spirit of good cheer, you understand. But letting the noisy minority in the NRA force us to allow this carnage to continue is just plain insane.

¹³ I do think gun nuts have a power hang-up. I don't know what is missing in their psyches that they need to feel they have the power to kill. But no sane society would allow this to continue.

¹⁴ Ban the damn things. Ban them all

¹⁵ You want protection? Get a dog.

 Thinking and Responding to the Reading

1. What is Ivins's main point (claim/argument)?
2. What evidence does she give to support her claim?
3. What counterarguments are offered?
4. What can you infer are Ivins's values concerning our civil liberties?
5. Define irony. Find two examples of irony in this reading and explain them.

The Gettysburg Address

Address delivered at the dedication of the cemetery at
Gettysburg, Pennsylvania
November 19, 1863

Abraham Lincoln

Activate Your Schema: What do you know about the American Civil War and the Battle of Gettysburg in particular? How should the living honor soldiers who died fighting? What people have you read about, heard about or perhaps even known who have sacrificed their lives for their country?

Vocabulary

conceived (par. 1)   consecrate (par. 3)   perish (par. 3)
proposition (par. 1)   hallow (par. 3)

1   Four score and seven years ago our fathers brought forth on this continent a new nation, conceived in liberty and dedicated to the proposition that all men are created equal.

2   Now we are engaged in a great civil war, testing whether that nation or any nation so conceived and so dedicated can long endure. We are met on a great battlefield of that war. We have come to dedicate a portion of that field as a final resting-place for those who here gave their lives that that nation might live. It is altogether fitting and proper that we should do this.

3   But in a larger sense, we cannot dedicate, we cannot consecrate, we cannot hallow this ground. The brave men, living and dead who struggled here have consecrated it far above our poor power to add or detract. The world will little note nor long remember what we say here, but it can never forget what they did here. It is for us the living rather to be dedicated here to the unfinished work which they who fought here have thus far so nobly advanced. It is rather for us to be here dedicated to the great task remaining before us—that from these honored dead we take increased devotion to that cause for which they gave the last full measure of devotion—that we here highly resolve that these dead shall not have died in vain, that this

nation under God shall have a new birth of freedom, and that
government of the people, by the people, for the people shall not
perish from the earth.

 Thinking and Responding to the Reading

1. What is the main idea of the Gettysburg Address?
2. What reasons does Lincoln offer to support his main idea?
3. What caused Lincoln to dedicate the cemetery at Gettysburg?
4. Explain why the Gettysburg Address is a prescriptive argument.
5. What is Lincoln implying when he said, "[We are] dedicated to the proposition that all men are created equal"?

Global Climate Change Impacts in the United States

The United States Global Change Research Program

Activate Your Schema: Think about various climate changes in our area. How do you think these changes will affect your activities?

Vocabulary

pose (par. 3)	adaptation (par. 4)	criteria (par. 9)
ozone (par. 3)	inundate (par. 6)	viable (par. 9)
sectors (par. 4)	infrastructure (par. 6)	

Overview of the Northeast

[1]   Climate changes are underway in the United States and are projected to grow. Climate-related changes are already observed in the United States and its coastal waters. These include increases in heavy downpours, rising temperature and sea level, rapidly retreating glaciers, thawing permafrost, lengthening growing seasons, lengthening ice-free seasons in the ocean and on lakes and rivers, earlier snowmelt, and alterations in river flows. These changes are projected to grow.

Trends

[2]   The annual average temperature in the Northeast has increased by 2°F since 1970, with winter temperatures rising twice this much. Warming has resulted in many other climate-related changes including more frequent very hot days, a longer growing season, an increase in heavy downpours, less winter precipitation falling as snow and more as rain, reduced snowpack, earlier break-up of winter ice on lakes and rivers, earlier spring snowmelt resulting in earlier peak river flows, rising sea surface temperatures, and rising sea level. These trends are projected to continue, with more dramatic changes under higher emissions scenarios compared to lower emissions scenarios. Some of the extensive climate-related changes

projected for the region could significantly alter the region's
economy, landscape, character, and quality of life.

Extreme heat and declining air quality

[3]   Extreme heat and declining air quality are likely to pose
increasing problems for human health, especially in urban areas. By
late this century under a higher emissions scenario, hot summer
conditions would arrive three weeks earlier and last three weeks
longer into fall. Northern cities, like Boston, would see a dramatic
increase in the number of days above 90 degrees. Cities that
currently experience just a few days above 100°F each summer
would average 20 such days per summer. Cities like Hartford and
Philadelphia would average nearly 30 days over 100°F per summer.
In addition, cities that now experience air quality problems would

Projected Days per Year over 90°F in Boston

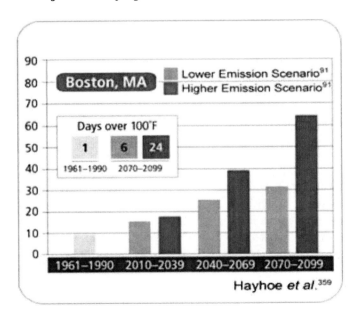

Hayhoe *et al.*[359]

see those problems worsen with rising temperatures, if no additional
controls were placed on ozone-causing pollutants.

Agricultural production adversely affected

4   Crop and livestock production will be increasingly challenged. Agriculture is considered one of the sectors most adaptable to changes in climate. However, increased heat, pests, water stress, diseases, and weather extremes will pose adaptation challenges for crop and livestock production. Agricultural production, including dairy, fruit, and maple syrup, is likely to be adversely affected as favorable climates shift. Large portions of the Northeast are likely to become unsuitable for growing popular varieties of apples, blueberries, and cranberries under a higher emissions scenario. The climate conditions suitable for maple/beech/birch forests are projected to shift dramatically northward, eventually leaving only a small portion of the Northeast with a maple-sugar business and the colorful fall foliage that is part of the region's iconic character.

Severe flooding more likely

5   Severe flooding due to sea-level rise and heavy downpours is likely to occur more frequently. The densely populated coasts of the Northeast face substantial increases in the extent and frequency of storm surge, coastal flooding, erosion, property damage, and loss of wetlands. New York State alone has more than $2.3 trillion in insured coastal property. Much of this coastline is exceptionally vulnerable to sea-level rise and related impacts.

6   With rising sea levels, a 100-year flood at the end of this century is projected to inundate a far larger area of New York City, especially under the higher emissions scenario. Critical transportation infrastructure located in the Battery area of lower Manhattan could be flooded far more frequently unless protected. The increased likelihood of flooding is causing planners to look into building storm-surge barriers in New York Harbor to protect downtown New York City.

Fisheries shift north and diminish

7   The center of lobster fisheries is projected to continue its northward shift, and the cod fishery on Georges Bank is likely to be diminished. Lobster catches in the southern part of the region have declined dramatically in the past decade, associated with a temperature-sensitive bacterial shell disease. Analyses also suggest

that lobster survival and settlement in northern regions of the Gulf of Maine could increase under warmer conditions, shifting the center of the lobster-fishing industry northward. Cod populations, also subject to over-fishing and other stresses, are likely to be adversely affected as temperatures continue to rise.

Reduction in snow cover

[8] The projected reduction in snow cover will adversely affect winter recreation and the industries that rely upon it. The length of the winter snow season would be cut in half across northern New York, Vermont, New Hampshire, and Maine, and reduced to just a week or two in southern parts of the region by late this century under a higher emissions scenario. Winter snow and ice sports, which contribute $7.6 billion annually to the region's economy, will be particularly affected by warming.

[9] The ski resorts in the Northeast have three climate-related criteria that need to be met for them to remain viable: the average length of the ski season must be at least 100 days; there must be a good probability of being open during the lucrative winter holiday week between Christmas and the New Year; and there must be enough nights that are sufficiently cold to enable snowmaking operations. By these standards, only one area in the region (not surprisingly, the one located farthest north) is projected to be able to support viable ski resorts by the end of this century under a higher emissions scenario.

Health impact

[10] Threats to human health will increase. Health impacts of climate change are related to heat stress, waterborne diseases, poor air quality, extreme weather events, and diseases transmitted by insects and rodents. Robust public health infrastructure can reduce the potential for negative impacts.

Future impact hinges on today's choices

[11] The amount and rate of future climate change depend primarily on current and future human-caused emissions of heat-trapping gases and airborne particles. Responses involve reducing emissions to limit future warming, and adapting to the changes that are unavoidable.

Thinking and Responding to the Reading

1. Cornell Note this article.
2. State the authors' overall argument. Indicate whether it is a prescriptive or descriptive argument. Use your Cornell Notes to answer this question.
3. Study the chart "Projected Days per Year over 100°F in Boston" and answer the following:
    a. From 1961-1990, how many days were over 90 degrees?
    b. Comparing 2040-2069 to 2070-2099, what is the change in the projected number of days above 90 degrees?
    c. Using your answer for 3b, what can you infer will change in people's daily lives?
    d. Looking at the bars in the graph, what can you infer about the effects of increased pollution controls on climate change?
    e. Compare the projections of 2010-2039 and 2070-2099. What can you infer?
    f. How many weeks of over-100-degree weather will occur in Boston in the 2070-2099 higher-emission scenario?

A Hanging

George Orwell

Activate Your Schema: Think about how prisoners should be punished and if race ever enters into how prisoners are treated. George Orwell, the pen name of Eric Blair, served in the Indian Imperial Police in Burma (present-day Myanmar) in the 1920s. "A Hanging" is from a collection of essays that reveal the behavior of the colonial officers and imperial rule in India.

Vocabulary

gallows (par. 2)	servile (par. 11)	garrulously (par. 20)
desolately (par. 3)	timorously (par. 15)	refractory (par. 22)
pariah (par. 6)	snigger (par. 17)	amicably (par. 24)

1   It was in Burma, sodden morning of the rains. A sickly light, like yellow tinfoil, was slanting over the high walls into the jail yard. We were waiting outside the condemned cells, a row of sheds fronted with double bars, like small animal cages. Each cell measured about ten feet by ten and was quite bare within except for a plank bed and a pot of drinking water. In some of them brown silent men were squatting at the inner bars, with their blankets draped round them. These were the condemned men, due to be hanged within the next week or two.

2   One prisoner had been brought out of his cell. He was a Hindu, a puny wisp of a man, with a shaven head and vague liquid eyes. He had a thick, sprouting moustache, absurdly too big for his body, rather like the moustache of a comic man on the films. Six tall Indian warders were guarding him and getting him ready for the gallows. Two of them stood by with rifles and fixed bayonets, while the others handcuffed him, passed a chain through his handcuffs and fixed it to their belts, and lashed his arms tight to his sides. They crowded very close about him, with their hands always on him in a careful, caressing grip, as though all the while feeling him to make sure he was there. It was like men handling a fish which is still alive and may jump back into the water. But he stood quite unresisting,

yielding his arms limply to the ropes, as though he hardly noticed what was happening.

3   Eight o'clock struck and a bugle call, desolately thin in the wet air, floated from the distant barracks. The superintendent of the jail, who was standing apart from the rest of us, moodily prodding the gravel with his stick, raised his head at the sound. He was an army doctor, with a grey toothbrush moustache and a gruff voice. "For God's sake hurry up, Francis," he said irritably. "The man ought to have been dead by this time. Aren't you ready yet?"

4   Francis, the head jailer, a fat Dravidian in a white drill suit and gold spectacles, waved his black hand. "Yes, sir; yes, sir," he bubbled. "All iss satisfactorily prepared. The hangman iss waiting. We shall proceed."

5   "Well, quick march, then. The prisoners can't get their breakfast till this job's over."

6   We set out for the gallows. Two warders marched on either side of the prisoner, with their rifles at the slope; two others marched close against him, gripping him by arm and shoulder, as though at once pushing and supporting him. The rest of us, magistrates and the like, followed behind. Suddenly, when we had gone ten yards, the procession stopped short without any order or warning. A dreadful thing happened—a dog came from goodness knows whence and appeared in the yard. It came bounding among us with a loud volley of barks and leapt round us, wagging its whole body, wild with glee at finding so many human beings together. It was a large woolly dog, half Airedale, half pariah. For a moment it pranced round us, and then, before anyone could stop it, it made a dash for the prisoner, and jumping up tried to lick his face. Everyone stood aghast, too taken aback even to grab at the dog.

7   "Who let that bloody brute in here?" said the superintendent angrily. "Catch it, someone!"

8   A warder, detached from the escort, charged clumsily after the dog, but it danced and gamboled just out of his reach, taking everything as part of the game. A young Eurasian jailer picked up a handful of gravel and tried to stone the dog away, but it dodged the stones and came after us again. Its yaps echoed from the jail walls. The prisoner, in the grasp of the two warders, looked on incuriously as though this was another formality of the hanging. It was several minutes before someone managed to catch the dog. Then we put my

83

handkerchief through its collar and moved off once more, with the
dog still straining and whimpering.

9   It was about forty yards to the gallows. I watched the bare
brown back of the prisoner marching in front of me. He walked
clumsily with his bound arms, but quite steadily, with that bobbing
gait of the Indian who never straightens his knees. At each step his
muscles slid neatly into place, the lock of hair on his scalp danced up
and down, his feet printed themselves on the wet gravel. And once,
in spite of the men who gripped him by each shoulder, he stepped
slightly aside to avoid a puddle on the path.

10   It is curious, but till that moment I had never realized what it
means to destroy a healthy, conscious man. When I saw the prisoner
step aside to avoid the puddle, I saw the mystery, the unspeakable
wrongness, of cutting a life short when it is in full tide. This man
was not dying; he was alive just as we were alive. All the organs of
his body were working—bowels digesting food, skin renewing itself,
nails growing, tissues forming—all toiling away in solemn foolery.
His nails would still be growing when he stood on the drop, when he
was falling through the air with a tenth of a second to live. His eyes
saw the yellow gravel and the grey walls, and his brain still
remembered, foresaw, reasoned—reasoned even about puddles. He
and we were a party of men walking together, seeing, hearing,
feeling, understanding the same world; and in two minutes, with a
sudden snap, one of us would be gone—one mind less, one world
less.

11   The gallows stood in a small yard, separate from the main
grounds of the prison, and overgrown with tall prickly weeds. It was
a brick erection like three sides of a shed, with planking on top, and
above that two beams and a crossbar with the rope dangling. The
hangman, a grey-haired convict in the white uniform of the prison,
was waiting beside his machine. He greeted us with a servile crouch
as we entered. At a word from Francis the two warders, gripping the
prisoner more closely than ever, half led, half pushed him to the
gallows and helped him clumsily up the ladder. Then the hangman
climbed up and fixed the rope round the prisoner's neck.

12   We stood waiting, five yards away. The warders had formed
in a rough circle round the gallows. And then, when the noose was
fixed, the prisoner began crying out to his god. It was a high,
reiterated cry of "Ram! Ram! Ram! Ram!"—not urgent and fearful

84

like a prayer or a cry for help, but steady, rhythmical, almost like the tolling of a bell. The dog answered the sound with a whine. The hangman, still standing on the gallows, produced a small cotton bag like a flour bag and drew it down over the prisoner's face. But the sound, muffled by the cloth, still persisted, over and over again: "Ram! Ram! Ram! Ram! Ram!"

13   The hangman climbed down and stood ready, holding the lever. Minutes seemed to pass. The steady, muffled crying from the prisoner went on and on, "Ram! Ram! Ram!"—never faltering for an instant. The superintendent, his head on his chest, was slowly poking the ground with his stick; perhaps he was counting the cries, allowing the prisoner a fixed number—fifty, perhaps, or a hundred. Everyone had changed colour. The Indians had gone grey like bad coffee, and one or two of the bayonets were wavering. We looked at the lashed, hooded man on the drop, and listened to his cries—each cry another sound of life; the same thought was in all our minds: oh, kill him quickly, get it over, stop that abominable noise!

14   Suddenly the superintendent made up his mind. Throwing up his head he made a swift motion with his stick. "Chalo!" he shouted almost fiercely.

15   There was a clanking noise, and then dead silence. The prisoner had vanished, and the rope was twisting on itself. I let go of the dog, and it galloped immediately to the back of the gallows; but when it got there it stopped short, barked, and then retreated into a corner of the yard, where it stood among the weeds, looking timorously out at us. We went round the gallows to inspect the prisoner's body. He was dangling with his toes pointed straight downwards, very slowly revolving, as dead as a stone.

16   The superintendent reached out with his stick and poked the bare body; it oscillated, slightly. "He's all right," said the superintendent. He backed out from under the gallows, and blew out a deep breath. The moody look had gone out of his face quite suddenly. He glanced at his wrist-watch. "Eight minutes past eight. Well, that's all for this morning, thank God."

17   The warders unfixed bayonets and marched away. The dog, sobered and conscious of having misbehaved itself, slipped after them. We walked out of the gallows yard, past the condemned cells with their waiting prisoners, into the big central yard of the prison. The convicts, under the command of warders armed with lathis, were

already receiving their breakfast. They squatted in long rows, each man holding a tin pannikin, while two warders with buckets marched round ladling out rice; it seemed quite a homely, jolly scene, after the hanging. An enormous relief had come upon us now that the job was done. One felt an impulse to sing, to break into a run, to snigger. All at once everyone began chattering gaily.

18   The Eurasian boy walking beside me nodded towards the way we had come, with a knowing smile: "Do you know, sir, our friend (he meant the dead man), when he heard his appeal had been dismissed, he pissed on the floor of his cell. From fright. Kindly take one of my cigarettes, sir. Do you not admire my new silver case, sir? From the boxwallah, two rupees, eight annas. Classy European style."

19   Several people laughed—at what, nobody seemed certain.

20   Francis was walking by the superintendent, talking garrulously. "Well, sir, all hass passed off with the utmost satisfactoriness. It wass all finished—flick! Like that. It is not always so—oah, no! I have known cases where the doctor wass obliged to go beneath the gallows and pull the prisoner's legs to ensure decease. Most disagreeable!"

21   "Wriggling about, eh? That's bad," said the superintendent.

22   "Ach, sir, it iss worse when they become refractory! One man, I recall, clung to the bars of hiss cage when we went to take him out. You will scarcely credit, sir, that it took six warders to dislodge him, three pulling at each leg. We reasoned with him. 'My dear fellow,' we said, 'think of all the pain and trouble you are causing to us!' But no, he would not listen! Ach, he was very troublesome!"

23   I found that I was laughing quite loudly. Everyone was laughing. Even the superintendent grinned in a tolerant way. "You'd better all come out and have a drink," he said quite genially. "I've got a bottle of whisky in the car. We could do with it."

24   We went through the big double gates of the prison, into the road. "Pulling at his legs!" exclaimed a Burmese magistrate suddenly, and burst into a loud chuckling. We all began laughing again. At that moment Francis's anecdote seemed extraordinarily funny. We all had a drink together, native and European alike, quite amicably. The dead man was a hundred yards away.

86

Thinking and Responding to the Reading

1. Is Orwell for or against capital punishment? How do you know this?
2. Who are the major characters?
3. What is the significance of the prisoner stepping around the puddle?
4. Orwell uses much figurative language, especially similes, in this essay. Find three similes in this essay and explain to what each simile refers.
5. At the end of the essay, in paragraphs 17-24, Orwell describes the behavior of the warden, superintendent and himself. What do you think Orwell is feeling? Then explain the last two sentences.

Annual Transmission Rates of Persons Living with HIV

United States Centers for Disease Control

Activate Your Schema: What do you know about HIV? How it is transmitted? How do you create meaning out of a chart?

Vocabulary
transmission (title)   diagnoses (par. 1)   perinatal (par. 4)

Diagnoses of HIV Infection by Age

[1]   Of the estimated number of new diagnoses of HIV infection in the 40 states with confidential name-based HIV infection reporting in 2009, the distribution of ages at time of diagnosis was as follows:

Age (Years)	Estimated Number of Diagnoses of HIV Infection, 2009
Under 13	166
Ages 13-14	21
Ages 15-19	2,036
Ages 20-24	6,237
Ages 25-29	5,951
Ages 30-34	5,020
Ages 40-44	5,519
Ages 45-49	4,865
Ages 50-54	3,323
Ages 55-59	2,004
Ages 60-64	900
Ages 65 or older	736

Diagnoses of HIV Infection by Race/Ethnicity

[2] CDC tracks diagnoses of HIV infection information on seven racial and ethnic groups: American Indian/Alaska Native; Asian; Black/African American; Hispanic/Latino; Native Hawaiian/Other Pacific Islander; White; and Multiple Races.

[3] In 2009, the **estimated number** of diagnoses of HIV infection in the 40 states with confidential name-based HIV infection reporting by race or ethnicity was as follows:

Race or Ethnicity	Estimated Number of Diagnoses of HIV Infection, 2009
American Indian/Alaska Native	189
Asian	470
Black/African American	21,652
Hispanic/Latino*	7,347
Native Hawaiian/Other Pacific Islander	34
White	11,803
Multiple Races	516

*Hispanics/Latinos can be of any race.

Diagnoses of HIV Infection by Transmission Category

[4] Six common transmission categories are male-to-male sexual contact, injection drug use, male-to-male sexual contact and injection drug use, heterosexual contact, mother-to-child (perinatal) transmission, and other (includes blood transfusions and unknown cause).

Following is the distribution of the **estimated number** of diagnoses of HIV infection among adults and adolescents in the 40 states with confidential name-based HIV infection reporting, by transmission category. A breakdown by sex is provided where appropriate.

Transmission Category	Estimated Number of Diagnoses of HIV Infection, 2009		
	Adult and Adolescent Males	Adult and Adolescent Females	Total
Male-to-male sexual contact	23,846	-	23,846
Injection drug use	2,449	1,483	3,932
Male-to-male sexual contact and injection drug use	1,131	-	1,131
Heterosexual contact*	4,399	8,461	12,860
Other**	47	29	76

* Heterosexual contact with a person known to have, or to be at high risk for, HIV infection.
** Includes hemophilia, blood transfusion, perinatal exposure, and risk not reported or not identified.

6   The distribution of the **estimated number** of diagnoses of HIV infection among children* in the 40 states with onfidential name-based HIV infection reporting by transmission category follows:

Transmission Category	Estimated Number of Diagnoses of HIV Infection, 2009
Perinatal	131
Other**	35

* The term "children" refers to persons under age 13 years at the time of diagnosis.

** Includes hemophilia, blood transfusion, and risk not reported or not identified.

Thinking and Responding to the Reading

1. What does HIV stand for? How is it different from AIDS?
2. Summarize each chart and explain what each means.
3. Who is at greatest risk for becoming infected with HIV? Who is at least risk?

Homemade Education
from *The Autobiography of Malcolm X*

Malcolm X

Activate Your Schema: How much discipline do you think it takes to change something about yourself? To copy an entire dictionary? To improve your reading?

Vocabulary

convey (par. 2	articulate (par. 2)	emulate (par. 4)
functional (par. 2)	envy (par. 4)	inevitable (par. 11)

¹   It was because of my letters that I happened to stumble upon starting to acquire some kind of homemade education.

²   I became increasingly frustrated at not being able to express what I wanted to convey in letters that I wrote, especially those to Mr. Elijah Muhammad. In the street, I had been the most articulate hustler out there—I had commanded attention when I said something. But now, trying to write simple English, I not only wasn't articulate, I wasn't even functional. How would I sound writing in slang, the way I would *say* it, something such as "Look, daddy, let me pull your coat about a cat, Elijah Muhammad—"

³   Many who today hear me somewhere in person, or on television, or those who read something I've said, will think I went to school far beyond the eighth grade. This impression is due entirely to my prison studies.

⁴   It had really begun back in Charlestown Prison, when Bimbi first made me feel envy of his stock of knowledge. Bimbi had always taken charge of any conversation he was in, and I had tried to emulate him. But every book I picked up had few sentences which didn't contain anywhere from one to nearly all of the words that might as well have been in Chinese. When I just skipped those words, of course, I really ended up with little idea of what the book said. So I had come to the Norfolk Prison Colony still going through only book-reading motions. Pretty soon, I would have quit even these motions unless I had received the motivation that I did.

⁵ I saw that the best thing I could do was get hold of a dictionary—to study to learn some words. I was lucky enough to reason also that I should try to improve my penmanship. It was sad. I couldn't even write in a straight line. It was both ideas together that moved me to request a dictionary along with some tablets and pencils from the Norfolk Prison Colony school.

⁶ I spent two days just riffling uncertainly through the dictionary's pages. I'd never realized so many words existed! I didn't know *which* words I needed to learn. Finally, just to start some kind of action, I began copying.

⁷ In my slow, painstaking, ragged handwriting, I copied into my tablet everything printed on that first page, down to the punctuation marks.

⁸ I believe it took me a day. Then, aloud, I read back, to myself, everything I'd written on the tablet. Over and over, aloud, to myself, I read my own handwriting.

⁹ I woke up the next morning, thinking about those words— immensely proud to realize that not only had I written so much at one time, but I'd written words that I never knew were in the world. Moreover, with a little effort, I also could remember what many of these words meant. I reviewed the words whose meanings I didn't remember. Funny thing, from the dictionary's first page right now, that "aardvark" springs to my mind. The dictionary had a picture of it, a long-tailed, long-eared, burrowing African mammal, which lives off termites caught by sticking out its tongue as an anteater does for ants.

¹⁰ I was so fascinated that I went on—I copied the dictionary's next page. And the same experience came when I studied that. With every succeeding page, I also learned of people and places and events from history. Actually the dictionary is like a miniature encyclopedia. Finally the dictionary's A section had filled a whole tablet—and I went on into the B's. That was the way I started copying what eventually became the entire dictionary. It went a lot faster after so much practice helped me to pick up handwriting speed. Between what I wrote in my tablet, and writing letters, during the rest of my time in prison I would guess I wrote a million words.

¹¹ I suppose it was inevitable that as my word-base broadened, I could for the first time pick up a book and read and now begin to understand what the book was saying. Anyone who has read a great

deal can imagine the new world that opened. Let me tell you something: from then until I left that prison, in every free moment I had, if I was not reading in the library, I was reading on my bunk. You couldn't have gotten me out of books with a wedge. Between Mr. Muhammad's teachings, my correspondence, my visitors—usually Ella and Reginald—and my reading of books, months passed without my even thinking about being imprisoned. In fact, up to then, I had never been so truly free in my life.

 Thinking and Responding to the Reading

1. Why did Malcolm X find himself frustrated while reading books and writing letters?
2. What method did he use to remedy his reading comprehension problems?
3. What did Malcolm X learn from the dictionary? Is the learning of individual words helpful to you in your reading comprehension? Explain.
4. What did Malcolm X realize when he read books in prison?
5. In paragraph 11, Malcolm X says, "In fact, up to then, I had never been so truly free in my life," and "Anyone who has read a great deal can imagine the new world that opened." Based on your own experience how has reading changed your life? If you haven't read something yet where your life has been changed, explain what impediments get in your way while reading; explain your struggle with reading in the same way that Malcolm X discusses his.

Housing Finance from the Great Depression to the Great Recession
from Reforming America's Housing Finance Market: A Report to Congress

United States Department of the Treasury and United States Department of Housing and Urban Development

Activate Your Schema: Have you ever taken out a loan from a bank or government institution? Do you know anyone who has a home mortgage?

Vocabulary

implementing (par. 1)	liquid market (par. 3)	capital (par. 5)
transparency (par. 1)	robust (par. 4)	conservatorship (par. 5)
benchmarks (par. 3)	lulled (par. 4)	decimated (par. 6)

[1] Nearly eighty years ago, in the midst of the Great Depression, the federal government began implementing sweeping reforms to the American financial system. These reforms—deposit insurance, limits on the risks banks can take, better transparency and investor protections in securities markets, a stronger Federal Reserve—helped build a financial system that provided a solid foundation for America's unprecedented prosperity.

[2] Improving how housing was financed was an important part of these broader Depression-era reforms. In the 1930s, following severe mortgage market disruptions, widespread foreclosures, and sinking homeownership rates, the government created the Federal Housing Administration ("FHA"), Fannie Mae, the Federal Home Loan Banks ("FHLBs") and, several decades later, Freddie Mac to help promote secure and sustainable home ownership for future generations of Americans.

[3] Fannie Mae and Freddie Mac held true to their original mission for many years. They established appropriate benchmarks for conforming loans that drove improved standards within the

broader mortgage industry. They helped reduce rates for borrowers by bringing transparency and standardization to the housing finance market. They played a central role in the development of securitization of conventional mortgages, which expanded access to homeownership for responsible borrowers, providing a much-needed link between places with established banking services and growing parts of the country without local funding sources for mortgages. For decades, borrowers, lenders, and investors benefited from the deep, liquid markets these institutions helped establish. This same marketplace gave American families access to simple, straightforward products, protecting them from sudden financial shocks and helping them build savings in their homes.

4   But in the years leading up to the recent financial crisis, trillions of dollars' worth of financial decisions were made across the U.S. economy and around the world on the faulty expectation that national house prices would only rise. Twenty years of economic stability had desensitized every player in the housing market to the possibility that home prices could fall. Indeed, despite occasional regional price declines, national home values in America had not declined on a consistent basis since the Depression. But in the years leading up to the recent crisis, a robust expansion in credit, fueled by processes and financial instruments designed to shift risk away from originators, combined with other factors, fed a rising demand for housing that lifted prices well above sustainable values. Average home values in many parts of the country skyrocketed. Mortgages became tools for speculative, short-term investments and a means to access easy cash. Lulled into a false sense of an ever-rising real estate market, some homebuyers took on more debt than they could afford to purchase homes beyond their means, and existing homeowners used their homes like ATM machines by converting home equity to cash.

5   By mid-2006, however, housing prices across a broad range of markets began to turn, eventually declining consistently for the first time since the 1930s. Almost no one in the housing finance market was prepared. Homeowners, investors, and financial institutions— including Fannie Mae and Freddie Mac—did not have enough capital supporting their investments to absorb the resulting losses. In 2008, credit markets froze. Our nation's financial system—which had outgrown and outmaneuvered a regulatory framework largely

designed in the 1930s—was driven to the brink of collapse. Millions of Americans lost their jobs, families lost their homes, and small businesses shut down. Fannie Mae and Freddie Mac experienced catastrophic losses and were placed into conservatorship, where they remain today.

6   The housing finance system must be reformed. It is the vital link to sustainable homeownership and rental options for millions of Americans, and it is central to our nation's economy. Its flaws were allowed to go unchecked for too long, contributing to a financial collapse that has strained families, decimated communities, and pushed the economy into the worst recession since the Great Depression. We need a path of reform, which will lead to a future system with more private capital, better-aligned incentives, more oversight, and less risk to the taxpayer—in short, to a healthier, more stable system of housing finance.

Thinking and Responding to the Reading

1. What is the main argument? Is it prescriptive, descriptive or both? Explain your answer with specifics from the reading.
2. Why were Fannie Mae and Freddie Mac created? List the reasons for their original mission.
3. According to the article, what are the causes of the latest financial crisis?
4. What are some of the effects of the crisis?
5. Explain the role of the federal government in ensuring that financial rules are in place for our protection.

How I Learned to Read and Write
from *Narrative of the Life of Frederick Douglass, An American Slave*

Frederick Douglass

Activate Your Schema: What connections can you make about reading and freedom?

Vocabulary

supercilious (par. 2)	exalted (par. 3)	discourse (par. 7)
petulance (par. 2)	exultingly (par. 5)	allayed (par. 7)
bated (par. 2)	preserve (par. 5)	resolute (par. 7)
impudent (par. 2)	chattels (par. 6)	amiable (par. 7)

1   Established in my new home in Baltimore, I was not very long in perceiving that in picturing to myself what was to be my life there, my imagination had painted only the bright side; and that the reality had its dark shades as well as its light ones. The open country which had been so much to me, was all shut out. Walled in on every side by towering brick buildings, the heat of the summer was intolerable to me, and the hard brick pavements almost blistered my feet. If I ventured out onto the streets, new and strange objects glared upon me at every step, and startling sounds greeted my ears from all directions. My country eyes and ears were confused and bewildered. Troops of hostile boys pounded upon me at every corner. They chased me, and called me "Eastern Shore man," till really I almost wished myself back on the Eastern Shore.

2   My new mistress happily proved to be all she had seemed, and in her presence I easily forgot all outside annoyances. Mrs. Sophia was naturally of an excellent disposition—kind, gentle, and cheerful. The supercilious contempt for the rights and feelings of others, and the petulance and bad humor which generally characterized slaveholding ladies, were all quite absent from her manner and bearing toward me. She had never been a slaveholder—a thing then quite unusual at the South—but had depended almost entirely upon

her own industry for a living. To this fact the dear lady no doubt owed the excellent preservation of her natural goodness of heart, for slavery could change a saint into a sinner, and an angel into a demon. I hardly knew how to behave toward "Miss Sopha," as I used to call Mrs. Hugh Auld. I could not approach her even as I had formerly approached Mrs. Thomas Auld. Why should I hang down my head, and speak with bated breath, when there was no pride to scorn me, no coldness to repel me, and no hatred to inspire me with fear? I therefore soon came to regard her as something more akin to a mother than a slaveholding mistress. So far from deeming it impudent in a slave to look her straight in the face, she seemed ever to say, "Look up, child; don't be afraid."

3   The sailors belonging to the sloop esteemed it a great privilege to be the bearers of parcels or messages to her, for whenever they came, they were sure of a most kind and pleasant reception. If little Thomas was her son, and her most dearly loved child, she made me something like his half-brother in her affections. If dear Tommy was exalted to a place on his mother's knee, "Freddy" was honored by a place at the mother's side. Nor did the slave boy lack the caressing strokes of her gentle hand, soothing him into the consciousness that, though motherless, he was not friendless. Mrs. Auld was not only kindhearted, but remarkably pious; frequent in her attendance of public worship, much given to reading the Bible, and to chanting hymns of praise when alone. Mr. Hugh was altogether a different character. He cared very little about religion; knew more of the world and was more a part of the world than his wife. He set out doubtless to be, as the world goes, a respectable man, and to get on by becoming a successful shipbuilder, in that city of shipbuilding. This was his ambition, and it fully occupied him. I was of course of very little consequence to him, and when he smiled upon me, as he sometimes did, the smile was borrowed from his lovely wife, and like all borrowed light, was transient, and vanished with the source whence it was derived. Though I must in truth characterize Master Hugh as a sour man of forbidding appearance, it is due to him to acknowledge that he was never cruel to me, according to the notion of cruelty in Maryland. During the first year or two, he left me almost exclusively to the management of his wife. He was my lawgiver.

4   In hands so tender as hers, and in the absence of the cruelties

of the plantation, I became both physically and mentally much more sensitive, and a frown from my mistress caused me far more suffering than had Aunt Katy's hardest cuffs. Instead of the cold, damp floor of my old master's kitchen, I was on carpets; for the corn bag in winter, I had a good straw bed, well furnished with covers; for the coarse cornmeal in the morning, I had good bread and mush occasionally; for my old, torn linen shirt, I had good clean clothes. I was really well off. My employment was to run errands, and to take care of Tommy, to prevent his getting in the way of carriages, and to keep him out of harm's way generally. So for a time everything went well. I say for a time, because the fatal poison of irresponsible power, and the natural influence of slave customs, were not very long in making their impression on the gentle and loving disposition of my excellent mistress. She regarded me at first as a child, like any other. This was the natural and spontaneous thought; afterwards, when she came to consider me as property, our relations to each other were changed, but a nature so noble as hers could not instantly become perverted, and it took several years before the sweetness of her temper was wholly lost.

5   The frequent hearing of my mistress reading the Bible aloud, for she often read aloud when her husband was absent, awakened my curiosity in respect to this mystery of reading, and roused in me the desire to learn. Up to this time I had known nothing whatever of this wonderful art, and my ignorance and inexperience of what it could do for me, as well as my confidence in my mistress, emboldened me to ask her to teach me to read. With an unconsciousness and inexperience equal to my own, she readily consented, and in an incredibly short time, by her kind assistance, I had mastered the alphabet and could spell words of three or four letters. My mistress seemed almost as proud of my progress as if I had been her own child, and supposing that her husband would be as well pleased, she made no secret of what she was doing for me. Indeed, she exultingly told him of the aptness of her pupil, and of her intention to persevere in teaching me, as she felt her duty to do, at least to read the Bible.

6   And here arose the first dark cloud over my Baltimore prospects, the precursor of chilling blasts and drenching storms. Master Hugh was astounded beyond measure, and probably for the first time proceeded to unfold to his wife the true philosophy of the slave system, and the peculiar rules necessary in the nature of the

case to be observed in the management of human chattels. Of course he forbade her to give me any further instruction, telling her in the first place that to do so was unlawful, as it was also unsafe; "for," said he, "if you give a nigger an inch he will take an ell. Learning will spoil the best nigger in the world. If he learns to read the Bible it will forever unfit him to be a slave. He should know nothing but the will of his master, and learn to obey it. As to himself, learning will do him no good, but a great deal of harm, making him disconsolate and unhappy. If you teach him how to read, he'll want to know how to write, and this accomplished, he'll be running away with himself."

7   Such was the tenor of Master Hugh's oracular exposition and it must be confessed that he very clearly comprehended the nature and the requirements of the relation of a master and slave. His discourse was the first decidedly antislavery lecture to which it had been my lot to listen. Mrs. Auld evidently felt the force of what he said, and like an obedient wife, began to shape her course in the direction indicated by him. The effect of his words on me was neither slight nor transitory. His iron sentences, cold and harsh, sunk like heavy weights deep into my heart, and stirred up within me a rebellion not soon to be allayed. This was a new and special revelation dispelling a painful mystery against which my youthful understanding had struggled, and struggled in vain, to wit, the white man's power to perpetuate the enslavement of the black man. "Very well," thought I. "Knowledge unfits a child to be a slave." I instinctively assented to the proposition, and from that moment I understood the direct pathway from slavery to freedom. It was just what I needed, and it came to me at a time and from a source whence I least expected it. Of course I was greatly saddened at the thought of losing the assistance of my kind mistress, but the information so instantly derived to some extent compensated me for the loss I had sustained in this direction. Wise as Mr. Auld was, he underrated my comprehension, and had little idea of the use to which I was capable of putting the impressive lesson he was giving to his wife. He wanted me to be a slave; I had already voted against that on the home plantation of Colonel Lloyd. That which he most loved I most hated; and the very determination which he expressed to keep me in ignorance only rendered me the more resolute to seek intelligence. In learning to read, therefore, I am not sure that I do not owe quite as

much to the opposition of my master as to the kindly assistance of my amiable mistress. I acknowledge the benefit rendered me by the one, and by the other, believing that but for my mistress I might have grown up in ignorance.

Thinking and Responding to the Reading

1. Define metaphor and simile. Find three metaphors and/or similes and explain their meanings.
2. How did Douglass's mistress, Mrs. Sopha, treat him? List examples from the text to support your answer.
3. Frederick Douglass was taught how to read by his mistress, Mrs. Sopha. What reasons did she give her husband for giving him reading instruction?
4. What was Master Hugh Auld's reaction to this news? Quote the lines which indicate his position towards teaching slaves to read.
5. What was Douglass's resolution after hearing Master Auld? Find the lines in the text to support your answer.
6. What did Douglass realize he must do to gain his freedom?

Marijuana: Weighing the Evidence

Carl Wellman

Activate Your Schema: Are you for or against legalizing marijuana?

Vocabulary

intrinsically (par. 1)	inhibit (par. 5)	analogy (par. 8)
hedonism (par. 1)	infer (par. 6)	tentatively (par. 9)
congenial (par. 3)	crucial (par. 7)	

1   What are we to say of the experience of smoking marijuana? After a little practice, most people find this experience very pleasant. The Le Dain Commission concluded that a major factor in the contemporary marijuana explosion in the adult population as well as among young people is the simple pleasure of the experience. For example, a teacher and mother of four testified, "When I smoke grass I do it in the same social way that I take a glass of wine at dinner or have a drink at a party. I do not feel that it is one of the great and beautiful experiences of my life; I simply feel that it is pleasant." Marijuana typically produces an experience free from anxiety, unusual in interesting ways, including intense sensations and emotions, and stimulating to the imagination. For these reasons it is no exaggeration to say that the experience is *very* pleasant. Since I believe that pleasure is intrinsically good, I conclude that the experience is good for its own sake.

2   I do not conclude, however, that it is very good for its own sake. Why not? It seems to me that traditional hedonism has misinterpreted the nature of valued experience because it has emphasized the role of feeling and ignored the element of significance in such experiences. If an experience feels good it is good (judged in itself and apart from its consequences), but the intensity of the feeling is no reliable measure of the degree of value. Most of the value or disvalue of our experiences comes from their significance or meaning. The experience of receiving an A on an exam feels good, but most of its value comes from the awareness that

103

this grade is the product of past effort and one step toward passing the course, earning a degree, and pursing a vocation. Only as one is aware of the place an experience has in the larger context of one's own life and the lives of others does the experience have any great value or disvalue. Because the experiences of smoking marijuana tend to be isolated from the mainstream of the user's life and to contribute very little to achieving personal goals or to advancing the welfare of others, these experiences, although very pleasant, are relatively meaningless. In my judgment, the experience of using marijuana usually has a genuine but very limited value.

3   For some young people, however, the experience of smoking marijuana is far from trivial. The use of marijuana represents a rejection of the competitive work ethic of their parents and the adoption of a very different ideal of life in which work should be intrinsically rewarding and not a mere means to material success. For them the good life consists more in shared enjoyments than in wealth and status gained at the expense of their competitors. Thus for many members of the drug subculture in our country, the use of marijuana offers far more than immediate and trivial pleasure; it provides a highly meaningful pleasure because it signifies both protest against an alien way of life and participation in a more congenial and more morally acceptable community. Nevertheless, since most of those who use marijuana do not belong to this drug subculture, it remains true that for most people the experience of smoking marijuana lacks this degree of intrinsic value.

4   What of the consequences of using marijuana? These vary considerably from case to case, but after predictions of the direst consequences and promises of easy salvation are discounted, two considerations remain before us. First, the use of marijuana releases one from the pressures of society and the anxieties deep within oneself. This immediate result is genuinely good, but it must be considered in the light of further consequences. Sometimes the use of marijuana will enable a person to live through a period of crisis or to endure a harsh environment without breaking down emotionally. It can sometimes supply a temporary relief from tensions that prepares the individual to return to reality and to cope with it. So far, so good. In other cases persons who turn to marijuana become psychologically dependent upon the drug. They may retreat into their dream world and become unable to face up to the problems they

must solve if they are to live a fully satisfactory life. Although these bad consequences probably occur in a relatively small minority of users, they are serious enough to constitute a real and considerable danger. It seems to me that the release afforded by the use of marijuana is sometimes beneficial and sometimes harmful; that the benefits are probably more common than the harms; but that the harm, when it does occur, is so great that it outweighs the benefits. On balance, I think it better to find less dangerous means to escape, or change, the harsh realities of our lives.

5   Second, marijuana is said to be a steppingstone to highly undesirable drugs like heroin or LSD. There is nothing necessary or inevitable in this progression. The person who uses marijuana is not psychologically compelled to go on to use heroin or LSD, and in fact the majority of those who smoke pot never even try these more dangerous drugs. Nevertheless, a significant minority of users do progress from marijuana to heroin or LSD, and I believe that their use of marijuana is one factor that predisposes them to use these other drugs. This seems to be so for several reasons. Most people in our society have been educated—or brainwashed—so that they are strongly inhibited about the use of drugs. When a person breaks through these inhibitions sufficiently to use marijuana, his inhibitions against the use of other drugs are also weakened. In addition, those who use drugs often form groups, even subcultures, within our society. Thus a person who begins to use marijuana may become associated with other drug users, some of whom use the much stronger drugs. This community of drug users provides ample opportunity and some social pressure at least to try other drugs.

6   Finally, because the sale and possession of marijuana are illegal, those who use marijuana must obtain their supply through the black market. In times when anti-marijuana laws are strongly enforced and supply is consequently diminished, there is evidence to suggest that users may turn to other available drugs—often more potent and harmful ones. The same persons who peddle marijuana often push heroin and LSD also. More- over, it is to their personal advantage to encourage their customers to progress to the stronger drugs. The heroin addict is a sure customer, and the user of more potent drugs can sometimes be charged very high prices. Since I believe that the use of marijuana leads, in a significant minority of cases, to the use of heroin or LSD, and since I believe that these

105

drugs are far worse than marijuana, I infer that the use of marijuana is, in this respect, undesirable.

7   Although the experience of using marijuana seems to have some positive value in itself, the use of marijuana seems to have more bad consequences than good ones. Everything considered, it seems to me that the use of marijuana under present conditions in our country is bad. The qualification "under present conditions" may well be crucial. That marijuana is sometimes a steppingstone to the use of more dangerous drugs seems to be due to the fact that users tend to form semi-isolated groups and that it can be obtained only on the black market. Both of these facts about our society probably stem in large measure from the fact that the use of marijuana is forbidden by law.

8   It is also possible that social conditions lie behind the frequency with which users of marijuana become psychologically dependent upon it. The fact that its use is socially condemned and practiced in groups of people who are often rather alienated from our society may be an important factor in turning users away from reality and making it hard for them to return to the normal pattern of life in our society. The analogy with alcohol, so often used in discussing drugs, may be enlightening here. Quite possibly the use of alcohol, whatever one may say of it today, was less good or more bad during Prohibition. The quality of booze was inferior, sometimes dangerously so, because much was made at home by those with limited knowledge and the rest was manufactured by people out for a quick profit. Again, those who drank during Prohibition tended to be the least law-abiding citizens, and buying liquor contributed to the financial resources of criminal organizations whose other activities were clearly harmful to society. Just as the repeal of Prohibition eliminated these socially conditioned disvalues of alcohol, so reforming the drug laws might significantly alter the harmful consequences of using marijuana.

9   The lesson to be learned, however, is not that marijuana is good. The most that can properly be inferred is that marijuana as used under present conditions in our country really is bad, and that some of its badness is conditioned by social factors. Until these factors change, I will continue to believe, somewhat tentatively, that the use of marijuana is undesirable.

Thinking and Responding to the Reading

1. What is Wellman's argument/conclusion? Is it prescriptive or descriptive?
2. Wellman explains the causes and effects of marijuana use. List the causes and their effects.
3. Explain whether Wellman uses inductive or deductive reasoning. Use the definition of induction and deduction to explain your answers.
4. What does Wellman say are the values of smoking marijuana? What values does he use as his counterargument?
5. What worldview perspectives does Wellman rely upon?

The Most Dangerous Game

Richard Connell

Activate Your Schema: What are your views on hunting? Does it matter if it's for sport or survival?

Vocabulary

indolently (par. 29)	ardent (par. 84)	droll (par. 114)
quarry (par.42)	debacle (par. 86)	imperative (par. 169)
aristocrat (par. 55)	imprudent (par. 86)	precariously (par. 177)
Cossack (par. 58)	condone (par. 113)	placid (par. 184)

1   "OFF THERE to the right—somewhere—is a large island," said Whitney." It's rather a mystery—"

2   "What island is it?" Rainsford asked.

3   "The old charts call it 'Ship-Trap Island,'" Whitney replied. "A suggestive name, isn't it? Sailors have a curious dread of the place. I don't know why. Some superstition—"

4   "Can't see it," remarked Rainsford, trying to peer through the dank tropical night that was palpable as it pressed its thick warm blackness in upon the yacht.

5   "You've good eyes," said Whitney, with a laugh, "and I've seen you pick off a moose moving in the brown fall bush at four hundred yards, but even you can't see four miles or so through a moonless Caribbean night."

6   "Nor four yards," admitted Rainsford. "Ugh! It's like moist black velvet."

7   "It will be light enough in Rio," promised Whitney. "We should make it in a few days. I hope the jaguar guns have come from Purdey's. We should have some good hunting up the Amazon. Great sport, hunting."

8   "The best sport in the world," agreed Rainsford.

9   "For the hunter," amended Whitney. "Not for the jaguar."

10   "Don't talk rot, Whitney," said Rainsford. "You're a big-game hunter, not a philosopher. Who cares how a jaguar feels?"

11   "Perhaps the jaguar does," observed Whitney.

12 "Bah! They've no understanding."

13 "Even so, I rather think they understand one thing—fear. The fear of pain and the fear of death."

14 "Nonsense," laughed Rainsford. "This hot weather is making you soft, Whitney. Be a realist. The world is made up of two classes—the hunters and the huntees. Luckily, you and I are hunters. Do you think we've passed that island yet?"

15 "I can't tell in the dark. I hope so."

16 "Why?" asked Rainsford.

17 "The place has a reputation—a bad one."

18 "Cannibals?" suggested Rainsford.

19 "Hardly. Even cannibals wouldn't live in such a God-forsaken place. But it's gotten into sailor lore, somehow. Didn't you notice that the crew's nerves seemed a bit jumpy today?"

20 "They were a bit strange, now you mention it. Even Captain Nielsen—"

21 "Yes, even that tough-minded old Swede, who'd go up to the devil himself and ask him for a light. Those fishy blue eyes held a look I never saw there before. All I could get out of him was 'This place has an evil name among seafaring men, sir.' Then he said to me, very gravely, 'Don't you feel anything?'—as if the air about us was actually poisonous. Now, you mustn't laugh when I tell you this—I did feel something like a sudden chill.

22 "There was no breeze. The sea was as flat as a plate-glass window. We were drawing near the island then. What I felt was a—a mental chill; a sort of sudden dread."

23 "Pure imagination," said Rainsford.

24 "One superstitious sailor can taint the whole ship's company with his fear."

25 "Maybe. But sometimes I think sailors have an extra sense that tells them when they are in danger. Sometimes I think evil is a tangible thing—with wave lengths, just as sound and light have. An evil place can, so to speak, broadcast vibrations of evil. Anyhow, I'm glad we're getting out of this zone. Well, I think I'll turn in now, Rainsford."

26 "I'm not sleepy," said Rainsford. "I'm going to smoke another pipe up on the afterdeck."

27 "Good night, then, Rainsford. See you at breakfast."

28 "Right. Good night, Whitney."

²⁹ There was no sound in the night as Rainsford sat there but the muffled throb of the engine that drove the yacht swiftly through the darkness, and the swish and ripple of the wash of the propeller. Rainsford, reclining in a steamer chair, indolently puffed on his favorite brier. The sensuous drowsiness of the night was on him." It's so dark," he thought, "that I could sleep without closing my eyes; the night would be my eyelids—"

³⁰ An abrupt sound startled him. Off to the right he heard it, and his ears, expert in such matters, could not be mistaken. Again he heard the sound, and again. Somewhere, off in the blackness, someone had fired a gun three times.

³¹ Rainsford sprang up and moved quickly to the rail, mystified. He strained his eyes in the direction from which the reports had come, but it was like trying to see through a blanket. He leaped upon the rail and balanced himself there, to get greater elevation; his pipe, striking a rope, was knocked from his mouth. He lunged for it; a short, hoarse cry came from his lips as he realized he had reached too far and had lost his balance. The cry was pinched off short as the blood-warm waters of the Caribbean Sea closed over his head.

³² He struggled up to the surface and tried to cry out, but the wash from the speeding yacht slapped him in the face and the salt water in his open mouth made him gag and strangle. Desperately he struck out with strong strokes after the receding lights of the yacht, but he stopped before he had swum fifty feet. A certain cool-headedness had come to him; it was not the first time he had been in a tight place. There was a chance that his cries could be heard by someone aboard the yacht, but that chance was slender and grew more slender as the yacht raced on. He wrestled himself out of his clothes and shouted with all his power. The lights of the yacht became faint and ever-vanishing fireflies; then they were blotted out entirely by the night.

³³ Rainsford remembered the shots. They had come from the right, and doggedly he swam in that direction, swimming with slow, deliberate strokes, conserving his strength. For a seemingly endless time he fought the sea. He began to count his strokes; he could do possibly a hundred more and then—

³⁴ Rainsford heard a sound. It came out of the darkness, a high

screaming sound, the sound of an animal in an extremity of anguish and terror.

35   He did not recognize the animal that made the sound; he did not try to; with fresh vitality he swam toward the sound. He heard it again; then it was cut short by another noise, crisp, staccato.

36   "Pistol shot," muttered Rainsford, swimming on.

37   Ten minutes of determined effort brought another sound to his ears—the most welcome he had ever heard—the muttering and growling of the sea breaking on a rocky shore. He was almost on the rocks before he saw them; on a night less calm he would have been shattered against them. With his remaining strength he dragged himself from the swirling waters. Jagged crags appeared to jut up into the opaqueness; he forced himself upward, hand over hand. Gasping, his hands raw, he reached a flat place at the top. Dense jungle came down to the very edge of the cliffs. What perils that tangle of trees and underbrush might hold for him did not concern Rainsford just then. All he knew was that he was safe from his enemy, the sea, and that utter weariness was on him. He flung himself down at the jungle edge and tumbled headlong into the deepest sleep of his life.

38   When he opened his eyes he knew from the position of the sun that it was late in the afternoon. Sleep had given him new vigor; a sharp hunger was picking at him. He looked about him, almost cheerfully.

39   "Where there are pistol shots, there are men. Where there are men, there is food," he thought. But what kind of men, he wondered, in so forbidding a place? An unbroken front of snarled and ragged jungle fringed the shore.

40   He saw no sign of a trail through the closely knit web of weeds and trees; it was easier to go along the shore, and Rainsford floundered along by the water. Not far from where he landed, he stopped.

41   Some wounded thing—by the evidence, a large animal—had thrashed about in the underbrush; the jungle weeds were crushed down and the moss was lacerated; one patch of weeds was stained crimson. A small, glittering object not far away caught Rainsford's eye and he picked it up. It was an empty cartridge.

42   "A twenty-two," he remarked. "That's odd. It must have been a fairly large animal too. The hunter had his nerve with him to tackle it

with a light gun. It's clear that the brute put up a fight. I suppose the first three shots I heard were when the hunter flushed his quarry and wounded it. The last shot was when he trailed it here and finished it."

43   He examined the ground closely and found what he had hoped to find—the print of hunting boots. They pointed along the cliff in the direction he had been going. Eagerly he hurried along, now slipping on a rotten log or a loose stone, but making headway; night was beginning to settle down on the island.

44   Bleak darkness was blacking out the sea and jungle when Rainsford sighted the lights. He came upon them as he turned a crook in the coast line, and his first thought was that he had come upon a village, for there were many lights. But as he forged along he saw to his great astonishment that all the lights were in one enormous building—a lofty structure with pointed towers plunging upward into the gloom. His eyes made out the shadowy outlines of a palatial chateau; it was set on a high bluff, and on three sides of it cliffs dived down to where the sea licked greedy lips in the shadows.

45   "Mirage," thought Rainsford. But it was no mirage, he found, when he opened the tall spiked iron gate. The stone steps were real enough; the massive door with a leering gargoyle for a knocker was real enough; yet above it all hung an air of unreality.

46   He lifted the knocker, and it creaked up stiffly, as if it had never before been used. He let it fall, and it startled him with its booming loudness. He thought he heard steps within; the door remained closed. Again Rainsford lifted the heavy knocker, and let it fall. The door opened then—opened as suddenly as if it were on a spring— and Rainsford stood blinking in the river of glaring gold light that poured out. The first thing Rainsford's eyes discerned was the largest man Rainsford had ever seen—a gigantic creature, solidly made and black bearded to the waist. In his hand the man held a long-barreled revolver, and he was pointing it straight at Rainsford's heart.

47   Out of the snarl of beard two small eyes regarded Rainsford.

48   "Don't be alarmed," said Rainsford, with a smile which he hoped was disarming. "I'm no robber. I fell off a yacht. My name is Sanger Rainsford of New York City."

49   The menacing look in the eyes did not change. The revolver pointing as rigidly as if the giant were a statue. He gave no sign that he understood Rainsford's words, or that he had even heard them.

He was dressed in uniform—a black uniform trimmed with gray astrakhan.

50   "I'm Sanger Rainsford of New York," Rainsford began again. "I fell off a yacht. I am hungry."

51   The man's only answer was to raise with his thumb the hammer of his revolver. Then Rainsford saw the man's free hand go to his forehead in a military salute, and he saw him click his heels together and stand at attention. Another man was coming down the broad marble steps, an erect, slender man in evening clothes. He advanced to Rainsford and held out his hand.

52   In a cultivated voice marked by a slight accent that gave it added precision and deliberateness, he said, "It is a very great pleasure and honor to welcome Mr. Sanger Rainsford, the celebrated hunter, to my home."

53   Automatically Rainsford shook the man's hand.

54   "I've read your book about hunting snow leopards in Tibet, you see," explained the man. "I am General Zaroff."

55   Rainsford's first impression was that the man was singularly handsome; his second was that there was an original, almost bizarre quality about the general's face. He was a tall man past middle age, for his hair was a vivid white, but his thick eyebrows and pointed military mustache were as black as the night from which Rainsford had come. His eyes, too, were black and very bright. He had high cheekbones, a sharp-cut nose, a spare, dark face—the face of a man used to giving orders, the face of an aristocrat. Turning to the giant in uniform, the general made a sign. The giant put away his pistol, saluted, withdrew.

56   "Ivan is an incredibly strong fellow," remarked the general, "but he has the misfortune to be deaf and mute. A simple fellow, but, I'm afraid, like all his race, a bit of a savage."

57   "Is he Russian?"

58   "He is a Cossack," said the general, and his smile showed red lips and pointed teeth. "So am I."

59   "Come," he said, "we shouldn't be chatting here. We can talk later. Now you want clothes, food, rest. You shall have them. This is a most-restful spot." Ivan had reappeared, and the general spoke to him with lips that moved but gave forth no sound.

60   "Follow Ivan, if you please, Mr. Rainsford," said the general. "I was about to have my dinner when you came. I'll wait for you.

You'll find that my clothes will fit you, I think."

61   It was to a huge, beam-ceilinged bedroom with a canopied bed big enough for six men that Rainsford followed the silent giant. Ivan laid out an evening suit, and Rainsford, as he put it on, noticed that it came from a London tailor who ordinarily cut and sewed for none below the rank of duke.

62   The dining room to which Ivan conducted him was in many ways remarkable. There was a medieval magnificence about it; it suggested a baronial hall of feudal times with its oaken panels, its high ceiling, its vast refectory tables where two-score men could sit down to eat. About the hall were mounted heads of many animals—lions, tigers, elephants, moose, bears; larger or more perfect specimens Rainsford had never seen. At the great table the general was sitting, alone.

63   "You'll have a cocktail, Mr. Rainsford," he suggested. The cocktail was surpassingly good; and, Rainsford noted, the table appointments were of the finest—the linen, the crystal, the silver, the china.

64   They were eating *borscht*, the rich, red soup with whipped cream so dear to Russian palates. Half apologetically General Zaroff said, "We do our best to preserve the amenities of civilization here. Please forgive any lapses. We are well off the beaten track, you know. Do you think the champagne has suffered from its long ocean trip?"

65   "Not in the least," declared Rainsford. He was finding the general a most thoughtful and affable host, a true cosmopolite. But there was one small trait of the general's that made Rainsford uncomfortable. Whenever he looked up from his plate he found the general studying him, appraising him narrowly.

66   "Perhaps," said General Zaroff, "you were surprised that I recognized your name. You see, I read all books on hunting published in English, French, and Russian. I have but one passion in my life, Mr. Rainsford, and it is the hunt."

67   "You have some wonderful heads here," said Rainsford as he ate a particularly well-cooked *filet mignon*. "That Cape buffalo is the largest I ever saw."

68   "Oh, that fellow. Yes, he was a monster."

69   "Did he charge you?"

70   "Hurled me against a tree," said the general. "Fractured my skull. But I got the brute."

71 "I've always thought," said Rainsford, "that the Cape buffalo is the most dangerous of all big game."

72 For a moment the general did not reply; he was smiling his curious red-lipped smile. Then he said slowly, "No. You are wrong, sir. The Cape buffalo is not the most dangerous big game." He sipped his wine. "Here in my preserve on this island," he said in the same slow tone, "I hunt more dangerous game."

73 Rainsford expressed his surprise. "Is there big game on this island?"

74 The general nodded. "The biggest."

75 "Really?"

76 "Oh, it isn't here naturally, of course. I have to stock the island."

77 "What have you imported, general?" Rainsford asked. "Tigers?"

78 The general smiled. "No," he said. "Hunting tigers ceased to interest me some years ago. I exhausted their possibilities, you see. No thrill left in tigers, no real danger. I live for danger, Mr. Rainsford."

79 The general took from his pocket a gold cigarette case and offered his guest a long black cigarette with a silver tip; it was perfumed and gave off a smell like incense.

80 "We will have some capital hunting, you and I," said the general. "I shall be most glad to have your society."

81 "But what game—" began Rainsford.

82 "I'll tell you," said the general. "You will be amused, I know. I think I may say, in all modesty, that I have done a rare thing. I have invented a new sensation. May I pour you another glass of port?"

83 "Thank you, General."

84 The general filled both glasses, and said, "God makes some men poets. Some He makes kings, some beggars. Me He made a hunter. My hand was made for the trigger, my father said. He was a very rich man with a quarter of a million acres in the Crimea, and he was an ardent sportsman. When I was only five years old he gave me a little gun, specially made in Moscow for me, to shoot sparrows with. When I shot some of his prize turkeys with it, he did not punish me; he complimented me on my marksmanship. I killed my first bear in the Caucasus when I was ten. My whole life has been one prolonged hunt. I went into the army—it was expected of noblemen's sons— and for a time commanded a division of Cossack cavalry, but my real interest was always the hunt. I have hunted every kind of game in

every land. It would be impossible for me to tell you how many animals I have killed."

85   The general puffed at his cigarette.

86   "After the debacle in Russia I left the country, for it was imprudent for an officer of the Czar to stay there. Many noble Russians lost everything. I, luckily, had invested heavily in American securities, so I shall never have to open a tearoom in Monte Carlo or drive a taxi in Paris. Naturally, I continued to hunt— grizzliest in your Rockies, crocodiles in the Ganges, rhinoceroses in East Africa. It was in Africa that the Cape buffalo hit me and laid me up for six months. As soon as I recovered I started for the Amazon to hunt jaguars, for I had heard they were unusually cunning. They weren't." The Cossack sighed. "They were no match at all for a hunter with his wits about him, and a high-powered rifle. I was bitterly disappointed. I was lying in my tent with a splitting headache one night when a terrible thought pushed its way into my mind. Hunting was beginning to bore me! And hunting, remember, had been my life. I have heard that in America businessmen often go to pieces when they give up the business that has been their life."

87   "Yes, that's so," said Rainsford.

88   The general smiled. "I had no wish to go to pieces," he said. "I must do something. Now, mine is an analytical mind, Mr. Rainsford. Doubtless that is why I enjoy the problems of the chase."

89   "No doubt, General Zaroff."

90   "So," continued the general, "I asked myself why the hunt no longer fascinated me. You are much younger than I am, Mr. Rainsford, and have not hunted as much, but you perhaps can guess the answer."

91   "What was it?"

92   "Simply this: hunting had ceased to be what you call 'a sporting proposition.' It had become too easy. I always got my quarry. Always. There is no greater bore than perfection."

93   The general lit a fresh cigarette.

94   "No animal had a chance with me anymore. That is no boast; it is a mathematical certainty. The animal had nothing but his legs and his instinct. Instinct is no match for reason. When I thought of this it was a tragic moment for me, I can tell you."

95   Rainsford leaned across the table, absorbed in what his host was saying.

116

[96] "It came to me as an inspiration what I must do," the general went on.

[97] "And that was?"

[98] The general smiled the quiet smile of one who has faced an obstacle and surmounted it with success. "I had to invent a new animal to hunt," he said.

[99] "A new animal? You're joking."

[100] "Not at all," said the general. "I never joke about hunting. I needed a new animal. I found one. So I bought this island built this house, and here I do my hunting. The island is perfect for my purposes—there are jungles with a maze of traits in them, hills, swamps—"

[101] "But the animal, General Zaroff?"

[102] "Oh," said the general, "it supplies me with the most exciting hunting in the world. No other hunting compares with it for an instant. Every day I hunt, and I never grow bored now, for I have a quarry with which I can match my wits."

[103] Rainsford's bewilderment showed in his face.

[104] "I wanted the ideal animal to hunt," explained the general. "So I said, 'What are the attributes of an ideal quarry?' And the answer was, of course, 'It must have courage, cunning, and, above all, it must be able to reason.'"

[105] "But no animal can reason," objected Rainsford.

[106] "My dear fellow," said the general, "there is one that can."

[107] "But you can't mean—" gasped Rainsford.

[108] "And why not?"

[109] "I can't believe you are serious, General Zaroff. This is a grisly joke."

[110] "Why should I not be serious? I am speaking of hunting."

[111] "Hunting? Great Guns, General Zaroff, what you speak of is murder."

[112] The general laughed with entire good nature. He regarded Rainsford quizzically. "I refuse to believe that so modern and civilized a young man as you seem to be harbors romantic ideas about the value of human life. Surely your experiences in the war—"

[113] "Did not make me condone cold-blooded murder," finished Rainsford stiffly.

[114] Laughter shook the general. "How extraordinarily droll you are!" he said. "One does not expect nowadays to find a young man of the

educated class, even in America, with such a naïve, and, if I may say so, mid-Victorian point of view. It's like finding a snuffbox in a limousine. Ah, well, doubtless you had Puritan ancestors. So many Americans appear to have had. I'll wager you'll forget your notions when you go hunting with me. You've a genuine new thrill in store for you, Mr. Rainsford."

115 "Thank you, I'm a hunter, not a murderer."

116 "Dear me," said the general, quite unruffled, "again that unpleasant word. But I think I can show you that your scruples are quite ill founded."

117 "Yes?"

118 "Life is for the strong, to be lived by the strong, and, if needs be, taken by the strong. The weak of the world were put here to give the strong pleasure. I am strong. Why should I not use my gift? If I wish to hunt, why should I not? I hunt the scum of the earth: sailors from tramp ships—lassars, blacks, Chinese, whites, mongrels—a thoroughbred horse or hound is worth more than a score of them."

119 "But they are men," said Rainsford hotly.

120 "Precisely," said the general. "That is why I use them. It gives me pleasure. They can reason, after a fashion. So they are dangerous."

121 "But where do you get them?"

122 The general's left eyelid fluttered down in a wink. "This island is called Ship Trap," he answered. "Sometimes an angry god of the high seas sends them to me. Sometimes, when Providence is not so kind, I help Providence a bit. Come to the window with me."

123 Rainsford went to the window and looked out toward the sea.

124 "Watch! Out there!" exclaimed the general, pointing into the night. Rainsford's eyes saw only blackness, and then, as the general pressed a button, far out to sea Rainsford saw the flash of lights.

125 The general chuckled. "They indicate a channel," he said, "where there's none; giant rocks with razor edges crouch like a sea monster with wide-open jaws. They can crush a ship as easily as I crush this nut." He dropped a walnut on the hardwood floor and brought his heel grinding down on it. "Oh, yes," he said, casually, as if in answer to a question, "I have electricity. We try to be civilized here."

126 "Civilized? And you shoot down men?"

127 A trace of anger was in the general's black eyes, but it was there

for but a second, and he said, in his most pleasant manner, "Dear me, what a righteous young man you are! I assure you I do not do the thing you suggest. That would be barbarous. I treat these visitors with every consideration. They get plenty of good food and exercise. They get into splendid physical condition. You shall see for yourself tomorrow."

128   "What do you mean?"

129   "We'll visit my training school," smiled the general. "It's in the cellar. I have about a dozen pupils down there now. They're from the Spanish bark *San Lucar* that had the bad luck to go on the rocks out there. A very inferior lot, I regret to say. Poor specimens and more accustomed to the deck than to the jungle." He raised his hand, and Ivan, who served as waiter, brought thick Turkish coffee. Rainsford, with an effort, held his tongue in check.

130   "It's a game, you see," pursued the general blandly. "I suggest to one of them that we go hunting. I give him a supply of food and an excellent hunting knife. I give him three hours' start. I am to follow, armed only with a pistol of the smallest caliber and range. If my quarry eludes me for three whole days, he wins the game. If I find him"—the general smiled—"he loses."

131   "Suppose he refuses to be hunted?"

132   "Oh," said the general, "I give him his option, of course. He need not play that game if he doesn't wish to. If he does not wish to hunt, I turn him over to Ivan. Ivan once had the honor of serving as official knouter to the Great White Czar, and he has his own ideas of sport. Invariably, Mr. Rainsford, invariably they choose the hunt."

133   "And if they win?"

134   The smile on the general's face widened. "To date I have not lost," he said. Then he added, hastily: "I don't wish you to think me a braggart, Mr. Rainsford. Many of them afford only the most elementary sort of problem. Occasionally I strike a tartar. One almost did win. I eventually had to use the dogs."

135   "The dogs?"

136   "This way, please. I'll show you."

137   The general steered Rainsford to a window. The lights from the windows sent a flickering illumination that made grotesque patterns on the courtyard below, and Rainsford could see moving about there a dozen or so huge black shapes; as they turned toward him, their eyes glittered greenly.

[138] "A rather good lot, I think," observed the general. "They are let out at seven every night. If anyone should try to get into my house—or out of it—something extremely regrettable would occur to him." He hummed a snatch of song from the *Folies Bergere*.

[139] "And now," said the general, "I want to show you my new collection of heads. Will you come with me to the library?"

[140] "I hope," said Rainsford, "that you will excuse me tonight, General Zaroff. I'm really not feeling well."

[141] "Ah, indeed?" the general inquired solicitously. "Well, I suppose that's only natural, after your long swim. You need a good, restful night's sleep. Tomorrow you'll feel like a new man, I'll wager. Then we'll hunt, eh? I've one rather promising prospect—" Rainsford was hurrying from the room.

[142] "Sorry you can't go with me tonight," called the general. "I expect rather fair sport—a big, strong, black. He looks resourceful—Well, good night, Mr. Rainsford; I hope you have a good night's rest."

[143] The bed was good, and the pajamas of the softest silk, and he was tired in every fiber of his being, but nevertheless Rainsford could not quiet his brain with the opiate of sleep. He lay, eyes wide open. Once he thought he heard stealthy steps in the corridor outside his room. He sought to throw open the door; it would not open. He went to the window and looked out. His room was high up in one of the towers. The lights of the chateau were out now, and it was dark and silent; but there was a fragment of sallow moon, and by its wan light he could see, dimly, the courtyard. There, weaving in and out in the pattern of shadow, were black, noiseless forms; the hounds heard him at the window and looked up, expectantly, with their green eyes. Rainsford went back to the bed and lay down. By many methods he tried to put himself to sleep. He had achieved a doze when, just as morning began to come, he heard, far off in the jungle, the faint report of a pistol.

[144] General Zaroff did not appear until luncheon. He was dressed faultlessly in the tweeds of a country squire. He was solicitous about the state of Rainsford's health.

[145] "As for me," sighed the general, "I do not feel so well. I am worried, Mr. Rainsford. Last night I detected traces of my old complaint."

[146] To Rainsford's questioning glance the general said, "Ennui. Boredom."

[147] Then, taking a second helping of *crêpes Suzette*, the general explained: "The hunting was not good last night. The fellow lost his head. He made a straight trail that offered no problems at all. That's the trouble with these sailors; they have dull brains to begin with, and they do not know how to get about in the woods. They do excessively stupid and obvious things. It's most annoying. Will you have another glass of *Chablis*, Mr. Rainsford?"

[148] "General," said Rainsford firmly, "I wish to leave this island at once."

[149] The general raised his thickets of eyebrows; he seemed hurt. "But, my dear fellow," the general protested, "you've only just come. You've had no hunting—"

[150] "I wish to go today," said Rainsford. He saw the dead black eyes of the general on him, studying him. General Zaroff's face suddenly brightened.

[151] He filled Rainsford's glass with venerable *Chablis* from a dusty bottle.

[152] "Tonight," said the general, "we will hunt—you and I."

[153] Rainsford shook his head. "No, general," he said. "I will not hunt."

[154] The general shrugged his shoulders and delicately ate a hothouse grape. "As you wish, my friend," he said. "The choice rests entirely with you. But may I not venture to suggest that you will find my idea of sport more diverting than Ivan's?"

[155] He nodded toward the corner to where the giant stood, scowling, his thick arms crossed on his hogshead of chest.

[156] "You don't mean—" cried Rainsford.

[157] "My dear fellow," said the general, "have I not told you I always mean what I say about hunting? This is really an inspiration. I drink to a foe worthy of my steel—at last." The general raised his glass, but Rainsford sat staring at him.

[158] "You'll find this game worth playing," the general said enthusiastically. "Your brain against mine. Your woodcraft against mine. Your strength and stamina against mine. Outdoor chess! And the stake is not without value, eh?"

[159] "And if I win—" began Rainsford huskily.

[160] "I'll cheerfully acknowledge myself defeated if I do not find you

by midnight of the third day," said General Zaroff. "My sloop will place you on the mainland near a town." The general read what Rainsford was thinking.

[161] "Oh, you can trust me," said the Cossack. "I will give you my word as a gentleman and a sportsman. Of course you, in turn, must agree to say nothing of your visit here."

[162] "I'll agree to nothing of the kind," said Rainsford.

[163] "Oh," said the general, "in that case—But why discuss that now? Three days hence we can discuss it over a bottle of *Veuve Cliquot*, unless—"

[164] The general sipped his wine.

[165] Then a businesslike air animated him. "Ivan," he said to Rainsford, "will supply you with hunting clothes, food, a knife. I suggest you wear moccasins; they leave a poorer trail. I suggest, too, that you avoid the big swamp in the southeast corner of the island. We call it Death Swamp. There's quicksand there. One foolish fellow tried it. The deplorable part of it was that Lazarus followed him. You can imagine my feelings, Mr. Rainsford. I loved Lazarus; he was the finest hound in my pack. Well, I must beg you to excuse me now. I always take a siesta after lunch. You'll hardly have time for a nap, I fear. You'll want to start, no doubt. I shall not follow till dusk. Hunting at night is so much more exciting than by day, don't you think? *Au revoir*, Mr. Rainsford, *au revoir*." General Zaroff, with a deep, courtly bow, strolled from the room.

[166] From another door came Ivan. Under one arm he carried khaki hunting clothes, a haversack of food, a leather sheath containing a long-bladed hunting knife; his right hand rested on a cocked revolver thrust in the crimson sash about his waist.

[167] Rainsford had fought his way through the bush for two hours. "I must keep my nerve. I must keep my nerve," he said through tight teeth.

[168] He had not been entirely clearheaded when the chateau gates snapped shut behind him. His whole idea at first was to put distance between himself and General Zaroff; and, to this end, he had plunged along, spurred on by the sharp rowers of something very like panic. Now he had got a grip on himself, had stopped, and was taking stock of himself and the situation. He saw that straight flight was futile; inevitably it would bring him face to face with the sea. He was in a

picture with a frame of water, and his operations, clearly, must take place within that frame.

[169] "I'll give him a trail to follow," muttered Rainsford, and he struck off from the rude path he had been following into the trackless wilderness. He executed a series of intricate loops; he doubled on his trail again and again, recalling all the lore of the fox hunt, and all the dodges of the fox. Night found him leg-weary, with hands and face lashed by the branches, on a thickly wooded ridge. He knew it would be insane to blunder on through the dark, even if he had the strength. His need for rest was imperative and he thought, "I have played the fox, now I must play the cat of the fable." A big tree with a thick trunk and outspread branches was nearby, and, taking care to leave not the slightest mark, he climbed up into the crotch, and, stretching out on one of the broad limbs, after a fashion, rested. Rest brought him new confidence and almost a feeling of security. Even so zealous a hunter as General Zaroff could not trace him there, he told himself; only the devil himself could follow that complicated trail through the jungle after dark. But perhaps the general was a devil—

[170] An apprehensive night crawled slowly by like a wounded snake and sleep did not visit Rainsford, although the silence of a dead world was on the jungle. Toward morning when a dingy gray was varnishing the sky, the cry of some startled bird focused Rainsford's attention in that direction. Something was coming through the bush, coming slowly, carefully, coming by the same winding way Rainsford had come. He flattened himself down on the limb and, through a screen of leaves almost as thick as tapestry, he watched....That which was approaching was a man.

[171] It was General Zaroff. He made his way along with his eyes fixed in utmost concentration on the ground before him. He paused, almost beneath the tree, dropped to his knees and studied the ground. Rainsford's impulse was to hurl himself down like a panther, but he saw that the general's right hand held something metallic—a small automatic pistol.

[172] The hunter shook his head several times, as if he were puzzled. Then he straightened up and took from his case one of his black cigarettes; its pungent incense-like smoke floated up to Rainsford's nostrils. Rainsford held his breath. The general's eyes had left the ground and were traveling inch by inch up the tree. Rainsford froze there, every muscle tensed for a spring. But the sharp eyes of the

hunter stopped before they reached the limb where Rainsford lay; a smile spread over his brown face. Very deliberately he blew a smoke ring into the air; then he turned his back on the tree and walked carelessly away, back along the trail he had come. The swish of the underbrush against his hunting boots grew fainter and fainter.

173   The pent-up air burst hotly from Rainsford's lungs. His first thought made him feel sick and numb. The general could follow a trail through the woods at night; he could follow an extremely difficult trail; he must have uncanny powers; only by the merest chance had the Cossack failed to see his quarry.

174   Rainsford's second thought was even more terrible. It sent a shudder of cold horror through his whole being. Why had the general smiled? Why had he turned back?

175   Rainsford did not want to believe what his reason told him was true, but the truth was as evident as the sun that had by now pushed through the morning mists. The general was playing with him! The general was saving him for another day's sport! The Cossack was the cat; he was the mouse. Then it was that Rainsford knew the full meaning of terror.

176   "I will not lose my nerve. I will not."

177   He slid down from the tree, and struck off again into the woods. His face was set and he forced the machinery of his mind to function. Three hundred yards from his hiding place he stopped where a huge dead tree leaned precariously on a smaller, living one. Throwing off his sack of food, Rainsford took his knife from its sheath and began to work with all his energy.

178   The job was finished at last, and he threw himself down behind a fallen log a hundred feet away. He did not have to wait long. The cat was coming again to play with the mouse.

179   Following the trail with the sureness of a bloodhound came General Zaroff. Nothing escaped those searching black eyes, no crushed blade of grass, no bent twig, no mark, no matter how faint, in the moss. So intent was the Cossack on his stalking that he was upon the thing Rainsford had made before he saw it. His foot touched the protruding bough that was the trigger. Even as he touched it, the general sensed his danger and leaped back with the agility of an ape. But he was not quite quick enough; the dead tree, delicately adjusted to rest on the cut living one, crashed down and struck the general a glancing blow on the shoulder as it fell; but for

his alertness, he must have been smashed beneath it. He staggered, but he did not fall; nor did he drop his revolver. He stood there, rubbing his injured shoulder, and Rainsford, with fear again gripping his heart, heard the general's mocking laugh ring through the jungle.

[180] "Rainsford," called the general, "if you are within sound of my voice, as I suppose you are, let me congratulate you. Not many men know how to make a Malay mancatcher. Luckily for me I, too, have hunted in Malacca. You are proving interesting, Mr. Rainsford. I am going now to have my wound dressed; it's only a slight one. But I shall be back. I shall be back."

[181] When the general, nursing his bruised shoulder, had gone, Rainsford took up his flight again. It was flight now, a desperate, hopeless flight, that carried him on for some hours. Dusk came, then darkness, and still he pressed on. The ground grew softer under his moccasins; the vegetation grew ranker, denser; insects bit him savagely.

[182] Then, as he stepped forward, his foot sank into the ooze. He tried to wrench it back, but the muck sucked viciously at his foot as if it were a giant leech. With a violent effort, he tore his feet loose. He knew where he was now. Death Swamp and its quicksand.

[183] His hands were tight closed as if his nerve were something tangible that someone in the darkness was trying to tear from his grip. The softness of the earth had given him an idea. He stepped back from the quicksand a dozen feet or so and, like some huge prehistoric beaver, he began to dig.

[184] Rainsford had dug himself in in France when a second's delay meant death. That had been a placid pastime compared to his digging now. The pit grew deeper; when it was above his shoulders, he climbed out and from some hard saplings cut stakes and sharpened them to a fine point. These stakes he planted in the bottom of the pit with the points sticking up. With flying fingers he wove a rough carpet of weeds and branches and with it he covered the mouth of the pit. Then, wet with sweat and aching with tiredness, he crouched behind the stump of a lightning-charred tree.

[185] He knew his pursuer was coming; he heard the padding sound of feet on the soft earth, and the night breeze brought him the perfume of the general's cigarette. It seemed to Rainsford that the general was coming with unusual swiftness; he was not feeling his way along, foot by foot. Rainsford, crouching there, could not see the general,

nor could he see the pit. He lived a year in a minute. Then he felt an impulse to cry aloud with joy, for he heard the sharp crackle of the breaking branches as the cover of the pit gave way; he heard the sharp scream of pain as the pointed stakes found their mark. He leaped up from his place of concealment. Then he cowered back. Three feet from the pit a man was standing, with an electric torch in his hand.

186 "You've done well, Rainsford," the voice of the general called. "Your Burmese tiger pit has claimed one of my best dogs. Again you score. I think, Mr. Rainsford, I'll see what you can do against my whole pack. I'm going home for a rest now. Thank you for a most amusing evening."

187 At daybreak Rainsford, lying near the swamp, was awakened by a sound that made him know that he had new things to learn about fear. It was a distant sound, faint and wavering, but he knew it. It was the baying of a pack of hounds.

188 Rainsford knew he could do one of two things. He could stay where he was and wait. That was suicide. He could flee. That was postponing the inevitable. For a moment he stood there, thinking. An idea that held a wild chance came to him, and, tightening his belt, he headed away from the swamp.

189 The baying of the hounds drew nearer, then still nearer, nearer, ever nearer. On a ridge Rainsford climbed a tree. Down a watercourse, not a quarter of a mile away, he could see the bush moving. Straining his eyes, he saw the lean figure of General Zaroff; just ahead of him Rainsford made out another figure whose wide shoulders surged through the tall jungle weeds; it was the giant Ivan, and he seemed pulled forward by some unseen force; Rainsford knew that Ivan must be holding the pack in leash.

190 They would be on him any minute now. His mind worked frantically. He thought of a native trick he had learned in Uganda. He slid down the tree. He caught hold of a springy young sapling and to it he fastened his hunting knife, with the blade pointing down the trail; with a bit of wild grapevine he tied back the sapling. Then he ran for his life. The hounds raised their voices as they hit the fresh scent. Rainsford knew now how an animal at bay feels.

191 He had to stop to get his breath. The baying of the hounds stopped abruptly, and Rainsford's heart stopped too. They must have reached the knife.

[192] He shinnied excitedly up a tree and looked back. His pursuers had stopped. But the hope that was in Rainsford's brain when he climbed died, for he saw in the shallow valley that General Zaroff was still on his feet. But Ivan was not. The knife, driven by the recoil of the springing tree, had not wholly failed.

[193] Rainsford had hardly tumbled to the ground when the pack took up the cry again.

[194] "Nerve, nerve, nerve!" he panted, as he dashed along. A blue gap showed between the trees dead ahead. Ever nearer drew the hounds. Rainsford forced himself on toward that gap. He reached it. It was the shore of the sea. Across a cove he could see the gloomy gray stone of the chateau. Twenty feet below him the sea rumbled and hissed. Rainsford hesitated. He heard the hounds. Then he leaped far out into the sea....

[195] When the general and his pack reached the place by the sea, the Cossack stopped. For some minutes he stood regarding the blue-green expanse of water. He shrugged his shoulders. Then he sat down, took a drink of brandy from a silver flask, lit a cigarette, and hummed a bit from *Madame Butterfly*.

[196] General Zaroff had an exceedingly good dinner in his great paneled dining hall that evening. With it he had a bottle of *Pol Roger* and half a bottle of *Chambertin*. Two slight annoyances kept him from perfect enjoyment. One was the thought that it would be difficult to replace Ivan; the other was that his quarry had escaped him; of course, the American hadn't played the game—so thought the general as he tasted his after-dinner liqueur. In his library he read, to soothe himself, from the works of Marcus Aurelius. At ten he went up to his bedroom. He was deliciously tired, he said to himself, as he locked himself in. There was a little moonlight, so, before turning on his light, he went to the window and looked down at the courtyard. He could see the great hounds, and he called, "Better luck another time," to them. Then he switched on the light.

[197] A man, who had been hiding in the curtains of the bed, was standing there.

[198] "Rainsford!" screamed the general. "How in God's name did you get here?"

[199] "Swam," said Rainsford. "I found it quicker than walking through the jungle."

[200] The general sucked in his breath and smiled. "I congratulate

you," he said. "You have won the game."

²⁰¹ Rainsford did not smile. "I am still a beast at bay," he said, in a low, hoarse voice. "Get ready, General Zaroff."

²⁰² The general made one of his deepest bows. "I see," he said. "Splendid! One of us is to furnish a repast for the hounds. The other will sleep in this very excellent bed. On guard, Rainsford...."

²⁰³ He had never slept in a better bed, Rainsford decided.

 Thinking and Responding to the Reading

1. Highlight four examples of foreshadowing in the story.
2. How does Rainsford feel about the animals he hunts at the beginning of the story? Highlight the changes you see in Rainsford's attitude towards hunting.
3. What inferences indicate that General Zaroff is a sophisticated man? Highlight the sentences that indicate this. *Hubris* means an overbearing pride or arrogance. How do you know that General Zaroff suffers from hubris?
4. What happens at the conclusion of the story, paragraphs 191-198? How is the ending of the story ironic?
5. What is the theme of the story?

The Necklace

Guy de Maupassaunt

Activate Your Schema: Are you envious of others who have more than you, or are you content with your life? What responsibility do you have when you borrow something?

Vocabulary

blunder (par. 1)	hierarchy (par. 2)	odious (par. 98)
dowry (par. 1)	caste (par. 3)	sou (par. 98)
caste (par. 2)	frugal (par. 23)	usury (par. 102)
ingenuity (par. 2)		

1   She was one of those pretty and charming girls, born by a blunder of destiny in a family of employees. She had no dowry, no expectations, no means of being known, understood, loved, married by a man rich and distinguished; and so she let them make a match for her with a little clerk in the Department of Education.

2   She dressed simply since she could not dress well; but she was unhappy as though kept out of her own class, as if fallen from a higher station; for women have no caste nor rank; their beauty, their grace, and their charm serve them instead of birth and fortune. Their natural ingenuity, their instinctive elegance, their flexibility of mind are their only hierarchy; and these make the daughters of the people the equals of the most lofty ladies.

3   Mathilde suffered intensely, feeling herself born for every delicacy and every luxury. She was distressed from the poverty of her dwelling, from the worn walls, the shabby chairs, the ugliness of the curtains. All these things, which another woman of her caste would not even have noticed, tortured her and made her indignant. The sight of the little peasant girl from Breton who did her humble housework awoke in her desolated regrets and distracted dreams. She let her mind dwell on the quiet vestibules, hung with Oriental tapestries, lighted by tall lamps of bronze, and on the two tall footmen in knee breeches who dozed in the large armchairs, made drowsy by the heat of the furnace. She let her mind dwell on the

large parlors, decked with old silk, with their delicate furniture, supporting precious bric-a-brac, and on the coquettish little rooms, perfumed, prepared for the five- o'clock chat with the most intimate friends, men well known and sought after, whose attentions all women envied and desired.

4   When she sat down to dine, before a tablecloth three days old, in front of her husband, who lifted the cover of the tureen, declaring with an air of satisfaction, "Ah, the good *pot-au-feu.* I don't know anything better than that," she was thinking of delicate repasts, with glittering silver, with tapestries peopling the walls with ancient figures and with strange birds in a fairy-like forest; she was thinking of exquisite dishes, served in marvelous platters, of compliments whispered and heard with a sphinx-like smile, while she was eating the rosy flesh of a trout or the wings of a quail. She had no gowns, no jewelry, nothing. And she loved nothing else; she felt herself made for that only. She would so much have liked to please, to be envied, to be seductive and sought after.

5   She had a rich friend, a former friend of her convent days, whom she did not want to go and see any more, so much did she feel sad as she came away. And she wept all day long, from chagrin, from regret, from despair, and from distress.

6   But one evening her husband came in with a proud air, holding in his hand a large envelope.

7   "There," said he, "there's something for you."

8   She quickly tore the paper and took out of it a printed card which bore these words:

9   "The Minister of Education and Mme. Georges Rampouneau beg M. and Mme. Loisel to do them the honor to pass the evening with them at the palace of the Ministry, on Monday, January 18."

10   Instead of being delighted, as her husband hoped, she threw the invitation on the table with annoyance, murmuring:—

11   "What do you want me to do with that?"

12   "But, my dear, I thought you would be pleased. You never go out, and here's a chance, a fine one. I had the hardest work to get it. Everybody is after them; they are greatly sought for and not many are given to the clerks. You will see there all the official world."

13   She looked at him with an irritated eye and she declared with impatience:—

14   "What do you want me to put on my back to go there?"

15   He had not thought of that; he hesitated:—

16   "But the dress in which you go to the theater. That looks very well to me—"

17   He stopped, astonished and distracted at seeing that his wife was weeping. Two big tears were descending slowly from the corners of the eyes to the corners of the mouth. He stuttered:—

18   "What's the matter? What's the matter?"

19   But by a violent effort she had conquered her trouble, and she replied in a calm voice as she wiped her damp cheeks:—

20   "Nothing. Only I have no clothes, and in consequence I cannot go to this party. Give your card to some colleague whose wife has a better outfit than I."

21   He was disconsolate. He began again:—

22   "See here, Mathilde, how much would this cost, a proper dress, which would do on other occasions; something very simple?"

23   She reflected a few seconds, going over her calculations, and thinking also of the sum which she might ask without meeting an immediate refusal and a frightened exclamation from the frugal clerk.

24   At last, she answered hesitatingly:—

25   "I don't know exactly, but it seems to me that with four hundred francs I might do it."

26   He grew a little pale, for he was reserving just that sum to buy a gun and treat himself to a little shooting, the next summer, on the plain of Nanterre, with some friends who used to shoot larks there on Sundays.

27   But he said:—

28   "All right. I will give you four hundred francs. But take care to have a pretty dress."

29   The day of the party drew near, and Mme. Loisel seemed sad, restless, anxious. Yet her dress was ready. One evening her husband said to her:—

30   "What's the matter? Come, now, you have been quite queer these last three days."

31   And she answered:—

32   "It annoys me not to have a jewel, not a single stone, to put on. I shall look poverty-stricken. I would almost rather not go to this party."

33   He answered:—

34   "You will wear some natural flowers. They are very stylish this time of the year. For ten francs you will have two or three magnificent roses."

35   But she was not convinced.

36   "No; there's nothing more humiliating than to look poor among other women who are rich."

37   But her husband cried:—

38   "What a goose you are! Go find your friend, Mme. Forester, and ask her to lend you some jewelry. You know her well enough to do that."

39   She gave a cry of joy:—

40   "That's true. I had not thought of it."

41   The next day she went to her friend's and told her about her distress.

42   Mme. Forester went to her mirrored wardrobe, took out a large chest, brought it, opened it, and said to Mme. Loisel:—

43   "Choose, my dear."

44   She saw at first bracelets, then a necklace of pearls, then a Venetian cross of gold set with precious stones of an admirable workmanship. She tried on the ornaments before the glass, hesitated, and could not decide to take them off and to give them up. She kept on asking:—

45   "You haven't anything else?"

46   "Yes, yes. Look. I do not know what you like."

47   All at once she discovered, in a box of black satin, a superb necklace of diamonds, and her heart began to beat with boundless desire. Her hands trembled in taking it up. She fastened it round her throat, on her high dress, and remained in ecstasy before herself.

48   Then, she asked, hesitating, full of anxiety:—

49   "Can you lend me this, only this?"

50   "Yes, yes, certainly."

51   She sprang to her friend's neck, kissed her with ardor, and then escaped with her treasure.

52   The day of the party arrived. Mme. Loisel was a success. She was the prettiest of them all, elegant, gracious, smiling, and mad with joy. All the men were looking at her, inquiring her name, asking to be introduced. All the attachés of the Cabinet wanted to dance with her. The Minister took notice of her.

53   She danced with delight, with passion, intoxicated with

pleasure, thinking of nothing, in the triumph of her beauty, in the glory of her success, in a sort of cloud of happiness made up of all these tributes, of all the admirations, of all these awakened desires, of this victory so complete and so sweet to a woman's heart.

54   She left the party about four in the morning. Since midnight, her husband had been dozing in a little anteroom with three other men whose wives were having a good time.

55   He threw over her shoulders the wraps he had brought to go home in, modest garments of every-day life, the poverty of which was out of keeping with the elegance of the ball dress. She felt this, and wanted to fly so as not to be noticed by the other women, who were wrapping themselves up in rich furs.

56   Loisel kept her back:—

57   "Wait a minute; you will catch cold outside; I'll call a cab."

58   But she did not listen to him, and went downstairs rapidly. When they were in the street, they could not find a carriage, and they set out in search of one, hailing the drivers whom they saw passing in the distance.

59   They went down toward the Seine, disgusted, shivering. Finally, they found on the Quai one of those old night-hawk cabs which one sees in Paris only after night has fallen, as though they are ashamed of their misery in the daytime.

60   It brought them to their door, rue des Martyrs; and they went up their own stairs sadly. For her it was finished. And he was thinking that he would have to be at the Ministry at ten o'clock.

61   She took off the wraps with which she had covered her shoulders, before the mirror, so as to see herself once more in her glory. But suddenly she gave a cry. She no longer had the necklace around her throat!

62   Her husband, half undressed already, asked:—

63   "What is the matter with you?"

64   She turned to him, terror-stricken:—

65   "I—I—I have not Mme. Forester's diamond necklace!"

66   He jumped up, frightened:—

67   "What? How? It is not possible!"

68   And they searched in the folds of the dress, in the folds of the wrap, in the pockets, everywhere. They did not find it.

69   He asked:—

70   "Are you sure you still had it when you left the ball?"

133

⁷¹ "Yes, I touched it in the vestibule of the Ministry."

⁷² "But if you had lost it in the street, we should have heard it fall. It must be in the cab."

⁷³ "Yes. That is probable. Did you take the number?"

⁷⁴ "No. And you—you didn't notice it?"

⁷⁵ "No."

⁷⁶ They gazed at each other, crushed. At last Loisel dressed himself again.

⁷⁷ "I'm going," he said, "back the whole distance we came on foot, to see if I cannot find it."

⁷⁸ And he went out. She stayed there, in her ball dress, without strength to go to bed, overwhelmed, on a chair, without a fire, without a thought.

⁷⁹ Her husband came back about seven o'clock. He had found nothing.

⁸⁰ Then he went to police headquarters, to the newspapers to offer a reward, to the cab company; he did everything, in fact, that a trace of hope could urge him to.

⁸¹ She waited all day, in the same dazed state in face of this horrible disaster.

⁸² Loisel came back in the evening, with his face worn and white; he had discovered nothing.

⁸³ "You must write to your friend," he said, "that you have broken the clasp of her necklace and that you are having it repaired. That will give us time to turn around."

⁸⁴ She wrote as he dictated.

⁸⁵ At the end of a week they had lost all hope. And Loisel, aged by five years, declared:—

⁸⁶ "We must see how we can replace those jewels."

⁸⁷ The next day they took the case which had held them to the jeweler whose name was in the cover. He consulted his books.

⁸⁸ "It was not I, madam, who sold this necklace. I only supplied the case."

⁸⁹ Then they went from jeweler to jeweler, looking for a necklace like the other, consulting their memory,—sick both of them with grief and anxiety.

⁹⁰ In a shop in the Palais Royal, they found a diamond necklace that seemed to them absolutely like the one they were seeking. It was priced at forty thousand francs. They could have it for thirty-six.

⁹¹ They begged the jeweler not to sell it for three days. And they made a bargain that he should take it back for thirty-four thousand, if the first was found before the end of February.

⁹² Loisel possessed eighteen thousand francs which his father had left him. He had to borrow the remainder.

⁹³ He borrowed, asking a thousand francs from one, five hundred from another, five here, three louis there. He gave promissory notes, made ruinous agreements, dealt with usurers, with all kinds of lenders. He compromised the end of his life, risked his signature without even knowing whether it could be honored; and, frightened by all the anguish of the future, by the black misery which was about to settle down on him, by the perspective of all sorts of physical deprivations and of all sorts of moral tortures, he went to buy the new diamond necklace, laying down on the jeweler's counter thirty-six thousand francs.

⁹⁴ When Mme. Loisel took back the necklace to Mme. Forester, the latter said, with an irritated air:—

⁹⁵ "You ought to have brought it back sooner, for I might have needed it."

⁹⁶ She did not open the case, which her friend had been fearing. If she had noticed the substitution, what would she have thought? What would she have said? Might she not have been taken for a thief?

⁹⁷ Mme. Loisel learned the horrible life of the needy. She made the best of it, moreover, frankly, heroically. The frightful debt must be paid. She would pay it. They dismissed the servant; they changed their rooms; they took an attic under the roof.

⁹⁸ She learned the rough work of the household, the odious labors of the kitchen. She washed the dishes, wearing out her pink nails on the greasy pots and the bottoms of the pans. She washed the dirty linen, the shirts and the towels, which she dried on a rope; she carried down the garbage to the street every morning, and she carried up the water, pausing for breath on every floor. And, dressed like a woman of the people, she went to the fruit-seller, the grocer, the butcher, a basket on her arm, bargaining, insulted, fighting for her wretched money, sou by sou.

⁹⁹ Every month they had to pay notes, to renew others to gain time.

¹⁰⁰ The husband worked in the evening keeping up the books of a

shopkeeper, and at night often he did copying at five sous the page.

^{101} And this life lasted ten years.

^{102} At the end of ten years they had paid everything back, everything, with the rates of usury and all the accumulation of heaped-up interest.

^{103} Mme. Loisel seemed aged now. She had become the robust woman, hard and rough, of a poor household. Badly combed, with her skirts awry and her hands red, her voice was loud, and she washed the floor with splashing water.

^{104} But sometimes, when her husband was at the office, she sat down by the window and she thought of that evening long ago, of that ball, where she had been so beautiful and so admired.

^{105} What would have happened if she had not lost that necklace? Who knows? Who knows? How singular life is, how changeable! What a little thing it takes to save you or to lose you.

^{106} Then, one Sunday, as she was taking a turn in the Champs Elysées, as a recreation after the labors of the week, she perceived suddenly a woman walking with a child. It was Mme. Forester, still young, still beautiful, still seductive.

^{107} Mme. Loisel felt moved. Should she speak to her? Yes, certainly. And now that she had paid up, she would tell her all. Why not?

^{108} She drew near.

^{109} "Good morning, Jeanne."

^{110} The other did not recognize her, astonished to be addressed thus familiarly by this plain woman of the people. She hesitated:—

^{111} "But—madam—I don't know—are you not making a mistake?"

^{112} "No. I am Mathilde Loisel."

^{113} Her friend gave a cry—

^{114} "Oh!—My poor Mathilde, how you are changed."

^{115} "Yes, I have had hard days since I saw you, poverty and many troubles,—and that because of you."

^{116} "Of me?—How so?"

^{117} "You remember that diamond necklace that you lent me to go to the ball at the Ministry?"

^{118} "Yes. And then?"

^{119} "Well, I lost it."

^{120} "How can that be?—since you brought it back to me?"

¹²¹ "I brought you back another just like it. And now for ten years we have been paying for it. You will understand that it was not easy for us, who had nothing. At last, it is done, and I am mighty glad."

¹²² Mme. Forester had guessed. "You say that you bought a diamond necklace to replace mine?"

¹²³ "Yes. You did not notice it, even, did you? They were exactly alike?"

¹²⁴ And she smiled with pride and naïve joy.

¹²⁵ Mme. Forester, much moved, took her by both hands—

¹²⁶ "Oh, my poor Mathilde. But mine were false. At most they were worth five hundred francs!"

 Thinking and Responding to the Reading

1. What the main idea of this story?
2. Describe Mme. Loisel's character at the beginning and at the end of the story. How does it change?
3. Describe M. Loisel's and the Mme. Forester's respective character traits.
4. How would you describe Mme. Loisel's decision making skills? What makes you think this?
5. Why is the story ironic? What clues in the story help you determine this?

137

Only Daughter

Sandra Cisneros

Activate Your Schema: Are you an only child or a sibling? Do you think being what you are affected the way you were brought up? Do you think most parents treat their sons and daughters the same?

Vocabulary

anthology (par. 1)	retrospect (par. 5)	bouts (par. 9)
destiny (par. 4)	philandering (par. 7)	vials (par. 18)

1   Once, several years ago, when I was just starting out my writing career, I was asked to write my own contributor's note for an anthology. I wrote: "I am the only daughter in a family of six sons. That explains everything."

2   Well, I've thought that ever since, and yes, it explains a lot to me, but for the reader's sake I should have written: "I am the only daughter in a Mexican family of six sons." Or even: "I am the only daughter of a Mexican father and a Mexican-American mother." Or: "I am the only daughter of a working-class family of nine." All of these had everything to do with who I am today.

3   I was/am the only daughter and only a daughter. Being an only daughter in a family of six sons forced me by circumstance to spend a lot of time by myself because my brothers felt it beneath them to play with a girl in public. But that aloneness, that loneliness, was good for a would-be-writer—it allowed me time to think and think, to imagine, to read and prepare myself.

4   Being only a daughter for my father meant my destiny would lead me to become someone's wife. That's what he believed. But when I was in the fifth grade and shared my plans for college with him, I was sure he understood. I remember by father saying. "*Que bueno, mi'ja*, that's good." That meant a lot to me, especially since my brothers thought the idea hilarious. What I didn't realize was that my father thought college was good for girls—good for finding a husband. After four years in college and two more in graduate

school, and still no husband, my father shakes his head even now and says I wasted all that education.

5   In retrospect, I'm lucky my father believed daughters were meant for husbands. It meant it didn't matter if I majored in something silly like English. After all, I'd find a nice professional eventually, right? This allowed me the liberty to putter about embroidering my little poems and stories without my father interrupting with so much as a "What's that you're writing?"

6   But the truth is, I wanted him to interrupt. I wanted my father to understand what it was I was scribbling, to introduce me as "My only daughter, the writer." Not as "This is my only daughter. She teaches." *Es maestro*—teacher. Not even *profesora*.

7   In a sense, everything I have ever written has been for him, to win his approval even though I know my father can't read English words, even though my father's only reading includes the brown-ink *Esto* sports magazines from Mexico City and the bloody *¡Alama!* magazines that feature yet another sighting of *La Virgen de Gaudalupe* on a tortilla or a wife's revenge on her philandering husband by bashing his skull in with a molcajete (a kitchen mortar made of volcanic rock). Or the *fotonovelas*, the little picture paperbacks with tragedy and trauma erupting from the characters' mouths in bubbles.

8   A father represents, then, the public majority. A public who is uninterested in reading, and yet one whom I am writing about and for, and privately trying to woo.

9   When we were growing up in Chicago, we moved a lot because of my father. He suffered bouts of nostalgia. Then we'd have to let go of our flat, store the furniture with mother's relatives, load the station wagon with baggage and bologna sandwiches and head south. To Mexico City.

10   We came back, of course. To yet another Chicago flat, another Chicago neighborhood, another Catholic school. Each time, my father would seek out the parish priest in order to get a tuition break, and complain or boast: "I have seven sons."

11   He meant *siete bijos*, seven children, but he translated it as "sons." "I have seven sons." To anyone who would listen. The Sears Roebuck employee who sold us the washing machine. The short-order cook where my father ate his ham-and-eggs breakfasts. "I have seven sons." As if he deserved a medal from the state.

[12] My papa. He didn't mean anything by the mistranslation. I'm sure. But somehow I could feel myself being erased. I'd tug my father's sleeve and whisper: "Not seven sons. Six! and one *daughter*."

[13] When my oldest brother graduated from medical school, he fulfilled my father's dream that we study hard and use this—our heads, instead of this—our hands. Even now my father's hands are thick and yellow, stubbed by a history of hammer and nails and twine and coils and springs. "Use this," my father said, tapping his head, "and not this," showing us those hands. He always looked tired when he said it.

[14] Wasn't college an investment? And hadn't I spent all those years in college? And if I didn't marry, what was it all for? Why would anyone go to college and then choose to be poor? Especially someone who had always been poor.

[15] Last year, after ten years of writing professionally, the financial rewards started to trickle in. My second National Endowment for the Arts Fellowship. A guest professorship at the University of California, Berkeley. My book, which sold to a major New York publishing house.

[16] At Christmas, I flew home to Chicago. The house was throbbing, same as always; hot tamales and sweet tamales hissing in my mother's pressure cooker, and everybody—my mother, six brothers, wives, babies, aunts, cousins—talking too loud and at the same time, like in a Fellini film, because that's just how we are.

[17] I went upstairs to my father's room. One of my stories had just been translated into Spanish and published in an anthology of Chicano writing, and I wanted to show it to him. Ever since he recovered from a stroke two years ago, my father likes to spend his leisure hours horizontally. And that's how I found him, watching a Pedro Infante movie on Galavision and eating rice pudding.

[18] There was a glass filled with milk on the bedside table. There were several vials of pills and balled Kleenex. And on the floor, one black sock and a plastic urinal that I didn't want to look at but looked at anyway. Pedro Infante was about to burst into song, and my father was laughing.

[19] I'm not sure if it was because my story was translated into Spanish, or because it was published in Mexico, or perhaps because the story dealt with Tepeyac, the *colonia* my father was raised in and

140

the house he grew up in, but at any rate, my father punched the mute button on his remote control and read my story.

20   I sat on the bed next to my father and waited. He read it very slowly. As if he were reading each line over and over. He laughed at all the right places and read lines he liked out loud. He pointed and asked questions: "Is this So-and-so?" "Yes," I said. He kept reading.

21   When he was finally finished, after what seemed like hours, my father looked up and asked: "Where can we get more copies of this for the relatives?"

22   Of all the wonderful things that happened to me last year, that was the most wonderful.

Thinking and Responding to the Reading

1. Why does Cisneros's father say he has "seven sons"? How does Cisneros say she benefitted from this? What are some other effects?
2. In paragraph 3 Cisneros says, "I was/am the only daughter and only a daughter." Explain the connotation of the quote.
3. Why does her father want to distribute copies of Cisneros's story to the family?
4. List "all the wonderful things" that happened to Cisneros in the year. Why does she write in paragraph 22, "Of all the wonderful things that happened to me last year, that was the most wonderful"?
5. What tone does Cisneros use in this memoir?

… Or a Childish Illusion of Justice?

Shelby Steele

Activate Your Schema: *Reparations* means to make amends for wrong or injury done. Congress has debated whether to give financial reparations to descendants of slaves. Do you think financial reparation for decedents of slaves is a good or bad idea?

Vocabulary

crucible (par. 2)	aristocratic (par. 3)	stagnated (par. 5)
scion (par. 3)	inertia (par. 5)	aggrieved (par. 6)

1   My father was born in the last year of the 19th century. His father was very likely born into slavery, though there are no official records to confirm this. Still, from family accounts, I can plausibly argue that my grandfather was born a slave.

2   When I tell people this, I worry that I may seem conceited, like someone claiming a connection to royalty. The extreme experience of slavery—its commitment to broken-willed servitude—was so intense a crucible that it must have taken a kind of genius to survive it. In the jaws of slavery and segregation, blacks created a life-sustaining form of worship, rituals for every human initiation from childbirth to death, a rich folk mythology, a world-famous written literature, a complete cuisine, a truth-telling comic sensibility and, of course, some of the most glorious music the world has ever known.

3   Like the scion of an aristocratic family, I mention my grandfather to stand a little in the light of the black American genius. So my first objection to reparation for slavery is that it feels like selling our birthright for a pot of porridge. There is a profound esteem that comes to us from having overcome four centuries of oppression.

4   This esteem is an irreplaceable resource. In Richard Wright's *Black Boy*, a black elevator operator makes pocket money by letting white men kick him in the behind for a quarter. Maybe reparations are not quite this degrading, but when you trade on the past victimization of your own people, you trade honor for dollars. And

this trading is only uglier when you are a mere descendent of those who suffered but nevertheless prevailed.

[5]   I believe the greatest problem black America has had over the past 30 years has been precisely a faith in reparational uplift—the idea that all the injustice we endured would somehow translate into the means of uplift. We fought for welfare programs that only subsidized human inertia, for cultural approaches to education that stagnated skill development in our young and for affirmative-action programs that removed the incentive to excellence in our best and brightest.

[6]   Today 70 percent of all black children are born out of wedlock. Sixty-eight percent of all violent crime is committed by blacks, most often against other blacks. Sixty percent of black fourth graders cannot read at grade level. And so on. When you fight for reparational uplift, you have to fit yourself into a victim-focused, protest identity that is at once angry and needy. You have to locate real transformative power in white society, and then manipulate white guilt by seducing it with neediness and threatening it with anger. And you must nurture in yourself, and pass on to your own children, a sense of aggrieved entitlement that sees black success as an impossibility without the intervention of white compassion.

[7]   The above statistics come far more from this rippling sense of entitlement than from racism. And now the demand for reparations is yet another demand for white responsibility when today's problem is a failure of black responsibility.

[8]   When you don't know how to go forward, you find an excuse to go backward. You tell yourself that if you just get a little justice for past suffering, you will feel better about the challenges you face. So you make justice a condition of your going forward. But of course, there is no justice for past suffering, and to believe there is only guarantees one's suffering.

[9]   The worst enemy black America faces today is not white racism but white guilt. This is what encourages us to invent new pleas rather than busy ourselves with the hard work of development. So willing are whites to treat us with deference that they are a hard mark to pass up. The entire civil-rights establishment strategizes to keep us the wards of white guilt. If these groups had to rely on black money rather than white corporate funding, they would all go under tomorrow.

[10]   An honest black leadership would portray our victimization as only a condition we faced, and nurture a black identity around the ingenuity by which we overcame it. It would see reparations as a childish illusion of perfect justice. I can't be repaid for my grandfather. The point is that I owe him a great effort.

 Thinking and Responding to the Reading

1. What is Steele's main idea?
2. List the reasons Steele uses to support his main idea.
3. Where does Steele use counter arguments to support his position?
4. What position does Steele want to see advocated by the black leadership?
5. What can you infer from the title's words "Illusion of Justice"?
6. Mykel Johnson's article "Forgiveness" discusses *teshuvah*, the concept that only the person who has been hurt can forgive. Discuss the concept of *teshuvah* as it relates to this essay.

The Power of Forgiveness

"Lewis"

Activate Your Schema: What are some harmful consequences that may result from anger toward someone whom you could forgive?

Vocabulary

prejudice (par. 1)   coincidentally (par. 7)   malice (par. 8)
haven (par. 3)   fashion (par. 8)

[1]   It was 12:37 a.m. as the bus pulled from the terminal at Bowling Green, Kentucky. The streets were silent and the night was cool. I'd gotten my sister on her way to Ft. Knox after a weekend visit. At this time, I wanted nothing more than to go back to the dorm and get some rest. I never thought that a trip to the bus station could be so dramatic, that I would face death because of others' prejudice. Later on, I would need to overcome the effects of that prejudice.

[2]   After giving my sister spending money, I couldn't afford to take a cab back to the dorm. So I decided to get a little exercise and run to the dorm, about four miles away. When I had gone about two blocks, I noticed a truck slowly following me. When I turned around to see who it was, the driver sped up, went to the next block, and turned right. After I'd run another couple blocks, I noticed the truck in front of me. A guy on the passenger side started yelling at me, "Hey, bootlip, rug head, nigger." However, I continued running, pretending to ignore him.

[3]   The guys took the next left as I continued jogging up the hill to the campus. Three blocks further on, they appeared again. This time, the driver had three other guys sitting in the back of the truck. "Nigger, we're going to kill you," they yelled as they threw cans and bottles at me. Trying not to show any fear, I continued my uphill journey to Western Kentucky University. By this time, I feared for my life and started praying silently to God. I knew that each step would bring me closer to a safe haven.

[4]   When the guys in the pickup took the next left, I passed them

by, and I didn't see or hear from them for three more blocks. However, as I approached the corner of the fourth block, they surprised me. Five white guys jumped from the corner and surrounded me. One guy wearing a University of Louisville baseball cap said to me, "Where ya' goin', Niggah?" and pushed me into a guy behind me. "Where'd ya steal that sweat suit?" Petrified beyond response, I bounced from one guy to another. Then the guy wearing the U. of L. hat hit me in the stomach. As I folded over, another guy kicked me in the side. Immediately after that blow, another kicked me hard in the rear, and then blows came from everywhere.

5   As I fell to the sidewalk, I felt a stick break on my back. There were more kicks to my face and ribs and then, I felt nothing.

6   When I awakened, my mother was sitting beside my bed. When she saw me move my head, she simply said, "Thank God." It took me three weeks to get out of the hospital, and seven more to recover from four broken ribs, a broken collarbone and arm, fractured skull, and severely beaten face. Physically, I did recover.

7   As people came to see me, I felt the tension between the blacks and whites. Coincidentally, the police reported that I was "assaulted by five unknown assailants," and left it at that. They failed to investigate either the vehicle or the license plate number that a witness reported.

8   When I got better, I purchased a .38 caliber handgun and walked the street every night for at least a month. I didn't speak to, eat with, or associate with white people in any form or fashion. One night, as I was walking away from the bus stop, I saw the pickup. As I waited for the driver to come out of the convenience store, the anger and hatred rose within me. All the malice I've ever felt transferred to the index finger of my right hand on the trigger of my .38.

9   When the guy came out of the store, I grabbed him from behind and jammed the gun in his side. I dragged him behind the building and put the gun to his throat. "Do you remember me?" I asked. "Uh…yeah," he answered. "Before I blow your brains out, I want to know why you all did that to me that night." When this man started to cry and plead for his life, I felt immensely powerful. However, he said, "I really am sorry, and I came to see you in the hospital. I'm the one who sent the card. 'Don't hate the whole white

race for the mistakes of the few....' I wrote that."

10   I remembered the card. As I looked at that man again, I saw the pain he had been carrying for four months. As I let up on the trigger, I looked at him and said, "I forgive you," and walked away. Then I took the bullets out of the gun and threw them to the ground.

11   As I walked up the hill to Western Kentucky University, each step gave me a new freedom. When I got to the top of the hill, I was a brand-new man. I was not only free of malice and prejudice; I had become a man who could forgive the prejudice of others. I had decided that night to walk in a new power, the power of forgiveness.

 Thinking and Responding to the Reading

1. List the observable descriptions of the narrator and his attackers.
2. What can you infer is different about the attacker who writes the card as compared to the other attackers?
3. What can you infer the victim feels once he "saw the pain [that his attacker] had been carrying?
4. What are the individual decisions that the narrator and his attackers face?
5. This essay is an enactment of Mykel Johnson's explanation of *teshuvah* in her essay "Forgiveness." How do the individual decisions of Lewis and the one attacker he speaks with exemplify *teshuvah*?
6. Johnson also differentiates between repentance and atonement. Does the attacker who wrote the note repent or atone? Explain your choice in a few sentences.

Remarks in Recognition
of the Artist

President John F. Kennedy

Activate Your Schema: Do artists (poets, artists, dancers, musicians) play a role in the way you think about your worldview?

Vocabulary

excerpt (prologue)	pieties (par. 1)	officious (par. 2)
humanities (prologue)	intrusive (par. 2)	polemic (par. 4)
platitudes (par. 1)		

PROLOGUE   *The following is an excerpt from a speech given by President John F. Kennedy on October 26, 1963, at Amherst College in Massachusetts in honor of the poet Robert Frost. Frost had died in January of that year. In this speech, President Kennedy made clear the need for a nation to represent itself not only through its strength but also through its art and, as he said, in "full recognition of the place of the artist." Two years later, President Lyndon Johnson signed the National Foundation on the Arts and the Humanities Act, creating The National Endowment for the Arts.*

1   Our national strength matters, but the spirit which informs and controls our strength matters just as much. This was the special significance of Robert Frost. He brought an unsparing instinct for reality to bear on the platitudes and pieties of society. His sense of the human tragedy fortified him against self-deception and easy consolation. "I have been" he wrote, "one acquainted with the night." And because he knew the midnight as well as the high noon, because he understood the ordeal as well as the triumph of the human spirit, he gave his age strength with which to overcome despair. At bottom, he held a deep faith in the spirit of man, and it is hardly an accident that Robert Frost coupled poetry and power, for he saw poetry as the means of saving power from itself. When power leads man towards arrogance, poetry reminds him of his limitations. When power

narrows the areas of man's concern, poetry reminds him of the richness and diversity of his existence. When power corrupts, poetry cleanses. For art establishes the basic human truth, which must serve as the touchstone of our judgment.

2   The artist, however faithful to his personal vision of reality, becomes the last champion of the individual mind and sensibility against an intrusive society and an officious state. The great artist is thus a solitary figure. He has, as Frost said, a lover's quarrel with the world. In pursuing his perceptions of reality, he must often sail against the currents of his time. This is not a popular role. If Robert Frost was much honored in his lifetime, it was because a good many preferred to ignore his darker truths. Yet in retrospect, we see how the artist's fidelity has strengthened the fibre of our national life.

3   If sometimes our great artists have been the most critical of our society, it is because their sensitivity and their concern for justice, which must motivate any true artist, makes him aware that our Nation falls short of its highest potential. I see little of more importance to the future of our country and our civilization than full recognition of the place of the artist.

4   If art is to nourish the roots of our culture, society must set the artist free to follow his vision wherever it takes him. We must never forget that art is not a form of propaganda; it is a form of truth. And as Mr. MacLeish once remarked of poets, there is nothing worse for our trade than to be in style. In free society art is not a weapon and it does not belong to the spheres of polemic and ideology. Artists are not engineers of the soul. It may be different elsewhere. But democratic society—in it, the highest duty of the writer, the composer, the artist is to remain true to himself and to let the chips fall where they may. In serving his vision of the truth, the artist best serves his nation. And the nation which disdains the mission of art invites the fate of Robert Frost's hired man, the fate of having "nothing to look backward to with pride, and nothing to look forward to with hope."

5   I look forward to a great future for America, a future in which our country will match its military strength with our moral restraint, its wealth with our wisdom, its power with our purpose. I look forward to an America which will not be afraid of grace and beauty, which will protect the beauty of our natural environment, which will preserve the great old American houses and squares and parks of our

national past, and which will build handsome and balanced cities for our future.

6   I look forward to an America which will reward achieve-ment in the arts as we reward achievement in business or statecraft. I look forward to an America which will steadily raise the standards of artistic accomplishment and which will steadily enlarge cultural opportunities for all of our citizens.

7   And I look forward to an America which commands respect throughout the world not only for its strength but for its civilization as well. And I look forward to a world which will be safe not only for democracy and diversity but also for personal distinction.

8   Robert Frost was often skeptical about projects for human improvement, yet I do not think he would disdain this hope. As he wrote during the uncertain days of the Second World War:

> *Take human nature altogether since time began . . .*
> *And it must be a little more in favor of man,*
> *Say a fraction of one percent at the very least . . .*
> *Our hold on this planet wouldn't have so increased.*

Because of Mr. Frost's life and work, because of the life and work of this college, our hold on this planet has increased.

 Thinking and Responding to the Reading

1. What is President Kennedy's argument in this speech given at Amherst College in 1963?
2. Is the argument inductive or deductive? Explain how.
3. President Kennedy lists many reasons and examples of the important role of poetry in our society. What are they?
4. Are President Kennedy's reasons you listed in question 3 valid? Use the test for soundness and validity to explain your answer.
5. After carefully analyzing this speech, explain why colleges and universities require all students to take humanities courses.

The Road Not Taken

Robert Frost

Activate Your Schema: What process do you use to make decisions? Have you ever wished you could choose more than one path when you have to make a decision?

Vocabulary
diverged (line 1)   undergrowth (line 5)   trodden (line 12)

1 Two roads diverged in a yellow wood,
2 And sorry I could not travel both
3 And be one traveler, long I stood
4 And looked down one as far as I could
5 To where it bent in the undergrowth;

6 Then took the other, as just as fair,
7 And having perhaps the better claim,
8 Because it was grassy and wanted wear;
9 Though as for that the passing there
10 Had worn them really about the same,

11 And both that morning equally lay
12 In leaves no step had trodden black,
13 Oh, I kept the first for another day!
14 Yet knowing how way leads on to way,
15 I doubted if I should ever come back.

16 I shall be telling this with a sigh
17 Somewhere ages and ages hence:
18 Two roads diverged in a wood, and I—
19 I took the one less traveled by,
20 And that has made all the difference.

Thinking and Responding to the Reading

1. What is Frost's main idea?
2. Frost uses the word "diverged" in the first line of this poem. Relate his use of "diverged" to divergent thinking in the creative thinking process.
3. The narrator settles on a choice. Which lines in the poem show his convergent thinking as it relates to the critical thinking process?
4. Explain in your own words the meaning of the following figurative phrases:
   a. "it bent in the undergrowth"
   b. "it was grassy and wanted wear"
   c. "in leaves no step had trodden black"

Salvation

Langston Hughes

Activate Your Schema: What are some of your experiences in a religious setting (church, temple, mosque, synagogue)? Have you ever felt pressure to conform to a religious practice?

Vocabulary

dire (par. 3)	rounder (par. 6)	serenely (par. 7)
gnarled (par. 4)	deacons (par. 6)	knickerbockered (par. 11)

[1]   I was saved from sin when I was going on thirteen. But not really saved. It happened like this. There was a big revival at my Auntie Reed's church. Every night for weeks there had been much preaching, singing, praying, and shouting, and some very hardened sinners had been brought to Christ, and the membership of the church had grown by leaps and bounds. Then just before the revival ended, they held a special meeting for children, "to bring the young lambs to the fold." My aunt spoke of it for days ahead. That night I was escorted to the front row and placed on the mourners' bench with all the other young sinners who had not yet been brought to Jesus.

[2]   My aunt told me that when you were saved you saw a light, and something happened to you inside! And Jesus came into your life! And God was with you from then on! She said you could see and hear and feel Jesus in your soul. I believed her. I had heard a great many old people say the same thing and it seemed to me they ought to know. So I sat there calmly in the hot, crowded church, waiting for Jesus to come to me.

[3]   The preacher preached a wonderful rhythmical sermon, all moans and shouts and lonely cries and dire pictures of hell, and then he sang a song about the ninety and nine safe in the fold, but one little lamb was left out in the cold. Then he said: "Won't you come? Won't you come to Jesus? You lambs, won't you come?" And he held out his arms to all us young sinners there on the mourners'

bench. And the little girls cried. And some of them jumped up and went to Jesus right away. But most of us just sat there.

4   A great many old people came and knelt around us and prayed, old women with jet-black faces and braided hair, old men with work-gnarled hands. And the church sang a song about the lower lights are burning, some poor sinners to be saved. And the whole building rocked with prayer and song.

5   Still I kept waiting to *see* Jesus.

6   Finally all the young people had gone to the altar and were saved, but one boy and me. He was a rounder's son named Westley. Westley and I were surrounded by sisters and deacons praying. It was very hot in the church, and getting late now. Finally Westley said to me in a whisper: "God damn! I'm tired o'sitting here. Let's get up and be saved." So he got up and was saved.

7   Then I was left all alone on the mourners' bench. My aunt came and knelt at my knees and cried, while prayers and song swirled all around me in the little church. The whole congregation prayed for me alone, in a mighty wail of moans and voices. And I kept waiting serenely for Jesus, waiting, waiting—but he didn't come. I wanted to see him, but nothing happened to me. Nothing! I wanted something to happen to me, but nothing happened.

8   I heard the songs and the minister saying: "Why don't you come? My dear child, why don't you come to Jesus? Jesus is waiting for you. He wants you. Why don't you come? Sister Reed, what is this child's name?"

9   "Langston," my aunt sobbed.

10   "Langston, why don't you come? Why don't you come and be saved? Oh, Lamb of God! Why don't you come?"

11   Now it was really getting late. I began to be ashamed of myself, holding everything up so long. I began to wonder what God thought about Westley, who certainly hadn't seen Jesus either, but who was now sitting proudly on the platform, swinging his knickerbockered legs and grinning down at me, surrounded by deacons and old women on their knees praying. God had not struck Westley dead for taking his name in vain or for lying in the temple. So I decided that maybe to save further trouble, I'd better lie, too, and say that Jesus had come, and get up and be saved.

12   So I got up.

13   Suddenly the whole room broke into a sea of shouting as they

saw me rise. Waves of rejoicing swept the place. Women leaped in the air. My aunt threw her arms around me. The minister took me by the hand and led me to the platform.

14   When things quieted down, in a hushed silence, punctuated by a few ecstatic "Amens," all the new young lambs were blessed in the name of God. Then joyous singing filled the room.

15   That night, for the first time in my life but one, for I was a big boy twelve years old—I cried. I cried, in bed alone and couldn't stop. I buried my head under the quilts, but my aunt heard me. She woke up and told my uncle I was crying because the Holy Ghost had come into my life, and because I had seen Jesus. But I was really crying because I couldn't bear to tell her that I had lied, that I had deceived everybody in the church, that I hadn't seen Jesus, and that now I didn't believe there was a Jesus anymore, since he didn't come to help me.

Thinking and Responding to the Reading

1.   What can you infer from the title?
2.   When Hughes writes about "lambs in the fold" and lambs in general, he is using a figure of speech, a comparison. What is being compared? Is it useful as a figure of speech?
3.   The words "sin" (par. 1), "mourner" (par. 1) and "salvation" (title) all have connotations. What are connotations and what connotations do these words have for you?
4.   Why does Westley "see" Jesus? Why does Hughes come to Jesus?
5.   Explain the irony in the last paragraph.

Sister Flowers

Maya Angelou

Activate Your Schema: Have you ever needed someone to help you change your life or make you feel special?

Vocabulary

sopped (par. 1)	sacrilegious (par. 17)	couched (par. 35)
benign (par. 4)	infuse (par. 24)	collective (par. 35)
unceremonious (par. 8)	leered (par. 32)	aura (par. 42)

1   For nearly a year, I sopped around the house, the Store, the school and the church, like an old biscuit, dirty and inedible. Then I met, or rather got to know, the lady who threw me my first life line.

2   Mrs. Bertha Flowers was the aristocrat of Black Stamps. She had the grace of control to appear warm in the coldest weather, and on the Arkansas summer days it seemed she had a private breeze which swirled around, cooling her. She was thin without the taut look of wiry people, and her printed voile dresses and flowered hats were as right for her as denim overalls for a farmer. She was our side's answer to the richest white woman in town.

3   Her skin was a rich black that would have peeled like a plum if snagged, but then no one would have thought of getting close enough to Mrs. Flowers to ruffle her dress, let alone snag her skin. She didn't encourage familiarity. She wore gloves too.

4   I don't think I ever saw Mrs. Flowers laugh, but she smiled often. A slow widening of her thin black lips to show even, small white teeth, then the slow effortless closing. When she chose to smile on me, I always wanted to thank her. The action was so graceful and inclusively benign.

5   She was one of the few gentlewomen I have ever known, and has remained throughout my life the measure of what a human being can be.

6   Momma had a strange relationship with her. Most often when she passed on the road in front of the Store, she spoke to Momma in that soft yet carrying voice, "Good day, Mrs. Henderson." Momma

responded with "How you, Sister Flowers?"

7   Mrs. Flowers didn't belong to our church, nor was she Momma's familiar. Why on earth did she insist on calling her Sister Flowers? Shame made me want to hide my face. Mrs. Flowers deserved better than to be called Sister. Then, Momma left out the verb. Why not ask, "How are you, Mrs. Flowers?" With the unbalanced passion of the young, I hated her for showing her ignorance to Mrs. Flowers. It didn't occur to me for many years that they were as alike as sisters, separated only by formal education.

8   Although I was upset, neither of the women was in the least shaken by what I thought an unceremonious greeting. Mrs. Flowers would continue her easy gait up the hill to her little bungalow, and Momma kept on shelling peas or doing whatever had brought her to the front porch.

9   Occasionally, though, Mrs. Flowers would drift off the road and down to the Store and Momma would say to me, "Sister, you go on and play." As I left I would hear the beginning of an intimate conversation, Momma persistently using the wrong verb, or none at all.

10   "Brother and Sister Wilcox is sho'ly the meanest—" "Is," Momma? "Is"? Oh, please, not "is," Momma, for two or more. But they talked, and from the side of the building where I waited for the ground to open up and swallow me, I heard the soft-voiced Mrs. Flowers and the textured voice of my grandmother merging and melting. They were interrupted from time to time by giggles that must have come from Mrs. Flowers (Momma never giggled in her life). Then she was gone.

11   She appealed to me because she was like people I had never met personally. Like women in English novels who walked the moors (whatever they were) with their loyal dogs racing at a respectful distance. Like the women who sat in front of roaring fireplaces, drinking tea incessantly from silver trays full of scones and crumpets. Women who walked over the "heath" and read morocco-bound books and had two last names divided by a hyphen. It would be safe to say that she made me proud to be Negro, just by being herself.

12   She acted just as refined as whitefolks in the movies and books and she was more beautiful, for none of them could have come near that warm color without looking gray by comparison.

¹³   I was fortunate that I never saw her in the company of powhitefolks. For since they tend to think of their whiteness as an evenizer, I'm certain that I would have had to hear her spoken to commonly as Bertha, and my image of her would have been shattered like the unmendable Humpty-Dumpty.

¹⁴   One summer afternoon, sweet-milk fresh in my memory, she stopped at the Store to buy provisions. Another Negro woman of her health and age would have been expected to carry the paper sacks home in one hand, but Momma said, "Sister Flowers, I'll send Bailey up to your house with these things."

¹⁵   She smiled that slow dragging smile, "Thank you, Mrs. Henderson. I'd prefer Marguerite, though." My name was beautiful when she said it. "I've been meaning to talk to her, anyway." They gave each other age-group looks.

¹⁶   Momma said, "Well, that's all right then. Sister, go and change your dress. You going to Sister Flowers's."

¹⁷   The chifforobe was a maze. What on earth did one put on to go to Mrs. Flowers's house? I knew I shouldn't put on a Sunday dress. It might be sacrilegious. Certainly not a house dress, since I was already wearing a fresh one. I chose a school dress, naturally. It was formal without suggesting that going to Mrs. Flowers's house was equivalent to attending church.

¹⁸   I trusted myself back into the Store.

¹⁹   "Now, don't you look nice." I had chosen the right thing, for once....

²⁰   There was a little path beside the rocky road, and Mrs. Flowers walked in front swinging her arms and picking her way over the stones.

²¹   She said, without turning her head, to me, "I hear you're doing very good school work, Marguerite, but that it's all written. The teachers report that they have trouble getting you to talk in class." We passed the triangular farm on our left and the path widened to allow us to walk together. I hung back in the separate unasked and unanswerable questions.

²²   "Come and walk along with me, Marguerite." I couldn't have refused even if I wanted to. She pronounced my name so nicely. Or more correctly, she spoke each word with such clarity that I was certain a foreigner who didn't understand English could have understood her.

23　　"Now no one is going to make you talk—possibly no one can. But bear in mind, language is man's way of communicating with his fellow man and it is language alone which separates him from the lower animals." That was a totally new idea to me, and I would need time to think about it.

24　　"Your grandmother says you read a lot. Every chance you get. That's good, but not good enough. Words mean more than what is set down on paper. It takes the human voice to infuse them with the shades of deeper meaning."

25　　I memorized the part about the human voice infusing words. It seemed so valid and poetic.

26　　She said she was going to give me some books and that I not only must read them, I must read them aloud. She suggested that I try to make a sentence sound in as many different ways as possible.

27　　"I'll accept no excuse if you return a book to me that has been badly handled." My imagination boggled at the punishment I would deserve if in fact I did abuse a book of Mrs. Flowers's. Death would be too kind and brief.

28　　The odors in the house surprised me. Somehow I had never connected Mrs. Flowers with food or eating or any other common experience of common people. There must have been an outhouse, too, but my mind never recorded it.

29　　The sweet scent of vanilla met us as she opened the door.

30　　"I made tea cookies this morning. You see, I had planned to invite you for cookies and lemonade so we could have this little chat. The lemonade is in the icebox."

31　　It followed that Mrs. Flowers would have ice on an ordinary day, when most families in our town bought ice late on Saturdays only a few times during the summer to be used in the wooden ice-cream freezers.

32　　She took the bags from me and disappeared through the kitchen door. I looked around the room that I had never in my wildest fantasies imagined I would see. Browned photographs leered or threatened from the walls and the white, freshly done curtains pushed against themselves and against the wind. I wanted to gobble up the room entire and take it to Bailey, who would help me analyze and enjoy it.

33　　"Have a seat, Marguerite. Over there by the table." She carried a platter covered with a tea towel. Although she warned that she hadn't tried her hand at baking sweets for some time, I was certain that like everything else about her the cookies would be perfect.

34 They were flat round wafers, slightly browned on the edges and butter-yellow in the center. With the cold lemonade they were sufficient for childhood's lifelong diet. Remembering my manners, I took nice little lady-like bites off the edges. She said she had made them expressly for me and that she had a few in the kitchen that I could take home to my brother. So I jammed one whole cake in my mouth and though crumbs scratched the insides of my jaws, and if I hadn't had to swallow, it would have been a dream come true.

35 As I ate she began the first of what we later called "my lessons in living." She said that I must always be intolerant of ignorance but understanding of illiteracy. That some people, unable to go to school, were more educated and even more intelligent than college professors. She encouraged me to listen carefully to what country people called mother wit. That in those homely sayings was couched the collective wisdom of generations.

36 When I finished the cookies she brushed off the table and brought a thick, small book from the bookcase. I had read *A Tale of Two Cities* and found it up to my standards as a romantic novel. She opened the first page and I heard poetry for the first time in my life.

37 "It was the best of times and the worst of times...." Her voice slid in and curved down through and over the words. She was nearly singing. I wanted to look at the pages. Were they the same that I had read? Or were there notes, music, lined on the pages, as in a hymn book? Her sounds began cascading gently. I knew from listening to a thousand preachers that she was nearing the end of her reading, and I hadn't really heard, heard to understand, a single word.

38 "How do you like that?"

39 It occurred to me that she expected a response. The sweet vanilla flavor was still on my tongue and her reading was a wonder in my ears. I had to speak.

40 I said, "Yes, ma'am." It was the least I could do, but it was the most also.

41 "There's one more thing. Take this book of poems and memorize one for me. Next time you pay me a visit, I want you to recite."

⁴² I have tried often to search behind the sophistication of years for the enchantment I so easily found in those gifts. The essence escapes but its aura remains. To be allowed, no, invited, into the private lives of strangers, and to share their joys and fears, was a chance to exchange the Southern bitter wormwood for a cup of mead with Beowulf or a hot cup of tea and milk with Oliver Twist. When I said aloud, "It is a far, far better thing that I do, than I have ever done…," tears of love filled my eyes at my selflessness.

⁴³ On that first day, I ran down the hill and into the road (few cars ever came along it) and had the good sense to stop running before I reached the Store.

⁴⁴ I was liked, and what a difference it made. I was respected not as Mrs. Henderson's grandchild or Bailey's sister but for just being Marguerite Johnson.

⁴⁵ Childhood's logic never asks to be proved (all conclusions are absolute). I didn't question why Mrs. Flowers had singled me out for attention, nor did it occur to me that Momma might have asked her to give me a little talking to. All I cared about was that she had made tea cookies for me and read to *me* from her favorite book. It was enough to prove that she liked me.

 Thinking and Responding to the Reading

1. Who is Sister Flowers and why does she choose to mentor Marguerite?
2. What can you infer from the relationship between Sister Flowers and Momma?
3. How does Marguerite come to appreciate Momma's wisdom?
4. To what do you attribute Marguerite's superior command of English?
5. Why does Marguerite admire Sister Flowers?
6. In paragraph 45, Angelou writes, "Childhood's logic never asks to be proved (all conclusions are absolute)." What does this mean? How is this different from adults' logic?

Sonnets 18 & 130

William Shakespeare

Activate Your Schema: Think about a letter, poem or song that expresses love.

N.B. When reading poetry, you only stop where there is punctuation. Stopping at the end of a line that doesn't contain punctuation often throws off the flow of the poem and hinders comprehension.

Sonnet 18

1	Shall I compare thee[0] to a summer's day?	you
2	Thou[0] art more lovely and more temperate.	you
3	Rough winds do shake the darling buds of May,	
4	And summer's lease hath[0] all too short a date.	has
5	Sometime too hot the eye of heaven shines,	
6	And often is his gold complexion dimmed.	
7	And every fair from fair sometime declines,	
8	By chance or nature's changing course untrimmed.	
9	But thy eternal summer shall not fade,	
10	Nor lose possession of that fair thou ow'st[0],	possess
11	Nor shall Death brag thou wander'st in his shade	
12	When in eternal lines to time thou grow'st.	
13	So long as men can breathe, or eyes can see,	
14	So long lives this, and this gives life to thee.	

Sonnet 130

1	My mistress'[0] eyes are nothing like the sun;	lover's
2	Coral is far more red than her lips' red;	
3	If snow be white, why then her breasts are dun[0];	gray
4	If hairs be wires, black wires grow on her head.	
5	I have seen roses damasked, red and white,	
6	But no such roses see I in her cheeks;	
7	And in some perfumes is there more delight	
8	Than in the breath that from my mistress reeks.	

⁹ I love to hear her speak, yet well I know
¹⁰ That music hath⁰ a far more pleasing sound;   has
¹¹ I grant I never saw a goddess go;
¹² My mistress, when she walks, treads on the ground:
¹³ And yet, by heaven, I think my love as rare
¹⁴ As any she belied with false compare.

Thinking and Responding to the Reading

1. Rewrite the poems line by line in modern English.
2. What is the main idea of each poem? Pay attention to the last two lines of each poem.
3. The last two lines in Shakespearean sonnets are called "the turn." Why do you think they are called this?
4. Shakespeare wrote these poems over 400 years ago. If you changed the language a little, could these poems have been written today? Why or why not?
5. Compare these poems. How are they similar and different?

from Teen Pregnancy in the United States

United States Centers for Disease Control

Activate Your Schema: Do you know anyone who became a parent before age 19? Do you think this parent and child have the same opportunities for a stable life as those who become parents after completing high school or college?

Vocabulary

incarceration (par. 2)   socioeconomic (par. 6)   trajectories (par. 6)
abstinence (par. 5)   comprise (par. 6)   disparities (par. 6)

1   More than 400,000 teen girls, aged 15-19 years, give birth each year in the US. The media often glamorize teens having sexual intercourse and teen parenting, but the reality is starkly different. Having a child during the teen years carries high costs—emotional, physical, and financial—to the mother, father, child, and community. Parents, educators, public health and medical professionals, and community organizations all have a role to play in reducing teen pregnancy.

The Importance of Prevention

2   Teen pregnancy and childbearing bring substantial social and economic costs through immediate and long-term impacts on teen parents and their children. Teen pregnancy accounts for more than $9 billion per year in costs to U.S. taxpayers for increased health care and foster care, increased incarceration rates among children of teen parents, and lost tax revenue because of lower educational attainment and income among teen mothers.

3   Pregnancy and birth are significant contributors to high school dropout rates among girls. Only about 50% of teen mothers receive a high-school diploma by age 22, versus nearly 90% of women who had not given birth during adolescence. The children of teenage

mothers are more likely to have lower school achievement and drop out of high school, have more health problems, be incarcerated at some time during adolescence, give birth as a teenager, and face unemployment as a young adult. These effects remain for the teen mother and her child even after adjusting for those factors that increased the teenager's risk for pregnancy, such as, growing up in poverty, having parents with low levels of education, growing up in a single-parent family, and having low attachment to and performance in school.

[4]   In 2009, a total of 409,840 infants were born to 15- 19 year olds, for a live birth rate of 39.1 per 1,000 women in this age group. Nearly two-thirds of births to women younger than age 18 and more than half of those among 18- 19 year olds are unintended. The US teen birth rate fell by more than one-third from 1991 through 2005, but then increased by 5 percent over two consecutive years. Data for 2008 and 2009, however, indicate that the long-term downward trend has resumed. The U.S. teen pregnancy and birth, sexually transmitted diseases (STDs), and abortion rates are substantially higher than those of other western industrialized nations.

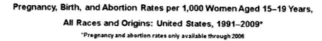

Pregnancy, Birth, and Abortion Rates per 1,000 Women Aged 15–19 Years,

All Races and Origins: United States, 1991–2009*

*Pregnancy and abortion rates only available through 2006

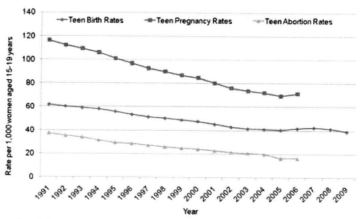

Reducing Teen Pregnancy and Promoting Health Equity Among Youth

[5]   Teen pregnancy prevention is one of the Centers for Disease Control's top six priorities, a "winnable battle" in public health and of paramount importance to health and quality of life for our youth. Evidence-based teen pregnancy prevention programs typically address specific protective factors on the basis of knowledge, skills, beliefs, or attitudes related to teen pregnancy:

1. Knowledge of sexual issues, HIV, other STDs, and pregnancy (including methods of prevention).
2. Perception of HIV risk.
3. Personal values about sex and abstinence.
4. Attitudes toward condoms (pro and con).
5. Perception of peer norms and behavior about sex.
6. Individual ability to refuse sex and to use condoms.
7. Intent to abstain from sex, or limit number of partners.
8. Communication with parents or other adults about sex, condoms, and contraception.
9. Individual ability to avoid HIV/STD risk and risk behaviors.
10. Avoidance of places and situations that might lead to sex.
11. Intent to use a condom.

[6]   Non-Hispanic black youth, Hispanic/Latino youth, American Indian/Alaska Native youth, and socio-economically disadvantaged youth of any race or ethnicity experience the highest rates of teen pregnancy and childbirth. Together, black and Hispanic youth comprise nearly 60% of U.S. teen births in 2009, although they represent only 35% of the total population of 15–19-year-old females. CDC is focusing on these priority populations because of the need for greater public health efforts to improve the life trajectories of adolescents facing significant health disparities, as well as to have the greatest impact on overall U.S. teen birth rates. Other priority populations for CDC's teen pregnancy prevention efforts include youth in foster care and the juvenile justice system, and otherwise living in conditions of risk.

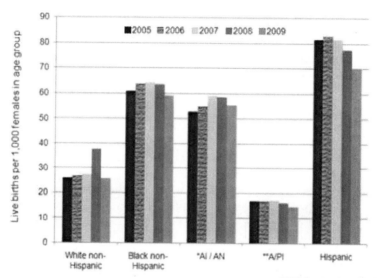

*AI/AN: American Indian/Alaska Native
**A/PI: Asian American/Pacific Islander

⁷   Sexual development is a normal part of the teen years. Teens need their parents' or an adult mentor's help in understanding their feelings, peer pressure, and how to say "no" if they do not want to have sex. If a teen starts having sex, he or she needs to know how to prevent pregnancy and sexually transmitted diseases. Teens want to talk with their parents or adult mentor about sex and relationships. Parents and adult mentors have a strong impact on whether a teenager makes healthy decisions for himself or herself. This goes for making healthy decisions about sex, as well. Research shows that teens who talk with their parents or adult mentor about sex, relationships, birth control and pregnancy—

- Begin to have sex at a later age.
- Use condoms and birth control more often if they do have sex.
- Have better communication with romantic partners.
- Have sex less often.

⁸   Parents and adult mentors can help children, pre-teens and teens make healthy choices about sex. Parents should talk to their

child, pre-teen, or teen early and often about healthy relationships, waiting to have sex, what happens as he or she grows, and other important topics.

[9]   During the past 20 years, the rate of teen girls having children has dropped by about 40% to its lowest level since records began being kept 70 years ago. Despite this good news, there is still much work to do, because teen pregnancy has such a huge impact on the future of America's children.

 Thinking and Responding to the Reading

1. What is the conclusion of the article?
2. According to the article, what are the consequences of teen pregnancy on the teen, the child and the nation?
3. What can you infer are the main causes of teen pregnancies among non-white teen populations?
4. What conclusions can you draw from the chart "Pregnancy, Birth, and Abortion Rates per 1,000 Women Ages 15-19 Years, All Races and Origins, 1991-2009"?
5. What conclusions can you draw from the chart "U.S. Birth Rates for Women Aged 15-19 Years by Race/Ethnicity 2005-2009"?

Quotes to Think About

"The paradox of education is precisely this: that as one begins to become conscious, one begins to examine the society in which he is being educated." James Baldwin

"I hear and I forget. I see and I remember. I do and I understand." Confucius

"You can practice shooting eight hours a day, but if your technique is wrong, then all you become is very good at shooting the wrong way. Get the fundamentals down, and the level of everything you do will rise." Michael Jordan

"Life is either a great adventure or nothing." Helen Keller

"We must become the change we want to see." Mahatma Gandhi

"What lies behind us and what lies before us are tiny matters compared to what lies within us." Ralph Waldo Emerson

"And as we let our own light shine, we unconsciously give other people permission to do the same." Nelson Mandela

"Friendship is a single soul dwelling in two bodies." Aristotle

"How wonderful it is that nobody need wait a single moment before starting to improve the world" Anne Frank

"Wise men talk because they have something to say; fools talk because they have to say something." Plato

"Turn your wounds into wisdom." Oprah Winfrey

"I was seldom able to see an opportunity until it had ceased to be one." Mark Twain

"Treat the earth well: it was not given to you by your parents, it was loaned to you by your children. We do not inherit the Earth from our ancestors, we borrow it from our children." Native American proverb

"A pessimist is one who makes difficulties of his opportunities and an optimist is one who makes opportunities of his difficulties." President Harry Truman

"I never paint dreams or nightmares. I paint my own reality." Frida Kahlo

"If you have integrity, nothing else matters. If you don't have integrity, nothing else matters." Senator Alan Simpson

"Mankind must remember that peace is not God's gift to his creatures; peace is our gift to each other." Elie Wiesel

Commonly Confused Words

advice	noun meaning opinion or counsel	**their**	belonging to them
advise	verb meaning to recommend	**there**	at that place; a neutral word used with verbs such as *is, are, were*
		they're	contracted shortened form of "they are"
affect	verb meaning to have influence		
effect	noun meaning a result		
all ready	completely prepared	**threw**	past tense of throw
already	previously; before	**through**	from one side to the other; finished
hear	perceive with the ear	**to**	a verb part, as in "to smile"; toward
here	in this place		
its	belonging to it	**too**	overly; also
it's	contraction of "it is" or "it has"	**two**	the number 2
knew	past tense of know	**your**	belonging to you
new	not old	**you're**	the shortened form of "you are"
passed	went by; succeeded in; handed to	**weather**	atmospheric condition
past	a time before the present	**whether**	if it happens that; in case; if
quiet	silent; hushed; still	**where**	in what place
quite	entirely; completely	**were**	past tense of the verb "to be"
		wear	to have on
sight	vision	**which**	what particular one or ones
cite	to quote or document	**witch**	a woman who practices sorcery
site	position or place		
than	shows comparison	**whose**	belonging to whom
then	next in time, space or order	**who's**	the shortened form of "who is" and "who has"